PRAISE FOR *SCHOOL, DISRUPTED*

If there were ever a perfect time to change the trajectory of our failed education system, it is now. And if there were ever a light to show the way, it's School, Disrupted.

—Debra Poneman

Best-selling author and award-winning speaker

Education is ready for disruption! After hundreds of years, it's time to reinvent how we teach our kids. Emily Greene does a spectacular job of giving us a vision of what is possible.

—Peter H. Diamandis, MD

Chairman and founder, XPRIZE; Singularity University
New York Times best-selling author of *Abundance*; *BOLD*; and *The Future Is Faster Than You Think*

You will devour every word! This book captures the raw fear of our predicament and offers beautiful insight, new perspective, and honest reflection about where we go from here to improve the school experience for our children.

—Day Halsey

Senior instructor in human development and family studies, Colorado State University

SCHOOL,
DISRUPTED

SCHOOL, DISRUPTED

DISRUPTED

Rediscovering the Joy of Learning
in a Pandemic-Stricken World

EMILY GREENE

Advantage®

Published by Advantage, Charleston, South Carolina.
Member of Advantage Media Group.

ADVANTAGE is a registered trademark, and the Advantage colophon is a trademark of Advantage Media Group, Inc.

Printed in the United States of America.

10 9 8 7 6 5 4 3 2 1

ISBN: 978-1-64225-243-9
LCCN: 2021900139

Cover design by David Taylor.
Layout design by Megan Elger.

This publication is designed to provide accurate and authoritative information in regard to the subject matter covered. It is sold with the understanding that the publisher is not engaged in rendering legal, accounting, or other professional services. If legal advice or other expert assistance is required, the services of a competent professional person should be sought.

 Advantage Media Group is proud to be a part of the Tree Neutral® program. Tree Neutral offsets the number of trees consumed in the production and printing of this book by taking proactive steps such as planting trees in direct proportion to the number of trees used to print books. To learn more about Tree Neutral, please visit **www.treeneutral.com**.

Advantage Media Group is a publisher of business, self-improvement, and professional development books and online learning. We help entrepreneurs, business leaders, and professionals share their Stories, Passion, and Knowledge to help others Learn & Grow. Do you have a manuscript or book idea that you would like us to consider for publishing? Please visit **advantagefamily.com** or call **1.866.775.1696**.

*To my parents, for teaching me to
never stop learning.*

*To my brother, for teaching me that
no industry is too big to be disrupted.*

*To my children, for teaching me more
than I could ever teach you.*

*To my husband, for teaching me that
true joy does not depend on circumstances.*

CONTENTS

THE DISRUPTION

Education is not the filling of a pail,
but the lighting of a fire.

—WILLIAM BUTLER YEATS

As the last seconds of 2020 ticked away, our family watched the televised New Year's Eve ball drop in Times Square. The empty streets in New York City and across the world reminded us of the pandemic's ongoing impact. Reflecting on the last year and all that the world has learned, hopefully the expression "hindsight is twenty-twenty" holds a deeper meaning. May we all face 2021 with a clearer understanding of how the disruption of school can lead to a better way to learn.

Last year, we rang in 2020 with the excitement of a new decade. It was, metaphorically, supposed to be the year of perfect twenty-twenty vision and clarity, not the year of disruption and ambiguity.

But in January and February of 2020, the coronavirus pandemic spread from China to Europe. By March, it had taken hold in the United States. Around spring break, school systems began to "temporarily" shut down in response to the fast-escalating rise in disease and the urgent need to stop the spread.

While justified, school closures felt abrupt and surreal. One day, our children rode school buses, attended classes, played sports, participated in activities, and spent time with friends. The next day, we were told to stay inside and socially isolate to protect our families and loved ones from this devastating virus.

Our lives came to a screeching halt, daily routines were upended, and school changed overnight. Suddenly homebound, children were forced into a jarringly different learning environment. Bedrooms became classrooms, pajamas became school uniforms, and teachers and peers became distant faces on computer screens. While our kids longed for normalcy, the worsening pandemic only brought more fear, isolation, and uncertainty. As the months wore on and schools stayed closed, it became evident that there would be no return to "normal" anytime soon. We all started to wonder: *What do we do now?*

LEARNING IN LOCKDOWN

During the shelter-in-place phase of the lockdown, I was walking outside and briefly spoke to a neighbor. Even though we both wore masks, and she stood on the other side of the street, I could feel her deep concern. She had four children under twelve who spent their school days chained to Zoom. She confided that she and her husband were overcome with worry about how the lockdown had taken a painful toll on their usually bright and playful children. The monotony and loneliness of distance learning had caused them to become moody and withdrawn. She described their emotional state in a way that brought tears to my eyes: the children's pilot lights had simply gone out.

So many parents can relate to this description. In the earliest days of the lockdown, millions of moms, dads, and caregivers watched their children grow anxious, depressed, and disengaged. It was clear that the abrupt switch to online learning sapped their mental, physical, and emotional energy.

As parents, we also struggled. The sudden closure of schools forced us to take on many new responsibilities, like supervising our children's remote learning. For families without a consistent or stable internet connection, trying to log in to Zoom or other digital classrooms and complete online schoolwork has been an ongoing nightmare, leaving some parents to wonder if their children are learning anything at all.

Some students have transitioned to hybrid learning, in which brick-and-mortar schools have slowly reopened their doors with restricted class sizes, one-way hallways, distanced desks, and required face coverings. Others have returned to school full-time with strict new safety requirements. In any of these situations, many families are still barely getting by as they juggle financial stresses with the added duties that come with the disruption of school.

WHEN WILL MY CHILD GO BACK TO SCHOOL?

As of January 2021, there are more than twenty million COVID-19 cases in the United States. Many cities are experiencing a spike in cases, and schools that reopened for hybrid or in-person learning are now reverting to a fully virtual model. While experts are optimistic about vaccines, most schools remain closed.

With this uncertainty, parents continue to struggle with a tough question: *When will my child go back to school?*

We do not know when the dust will settle—and we do not know what the world will look like when it does. What we do know is that the coronavirus pandemic is a disruption of epic proportions, changing how our children are educated in ways we never predicted.

While change is hard, I absolutely believe that this disruption brings a once-in-a-generation opportunity to improve our nineteenth-century education system. Just as we traded in the horse and carriage for the automobile, cross-country trains for cross-country planes, and analog phones for life-changing microchips, this disruption is our chance to trade in our outdated education system for something better, to shift our mindsets, and to rekindle our children's joy of learning from the inside out.

That is why I wrote this book, to offer an uplifting, achievable way for parents, caregivers, and educators to help children rediscover the joy of learning in this pandemic-stricken world. I do not aim to solve all of the challenges related to distance learning or tackle big issues like equity and access. Instead, I share a perspective on how this disruption can become a moment of transformation, helping our children come away from this difficult period with a new mindset.

It often takes a seismic disruption to change the way things have always been done.

It often takes a seismic disruption to change the way things have always been done. Before the pandemic, I jokingly said that it would take a cata-clysmic world event, like an alien invasion, to truly disrupt education. While I could have never predicted this worldwide pandemic, its absolute disruption of school will change education forever and be studied in the history books for generations to come.

As the saying goes, it is darkest before the dawn. In this global health crisis, we have learned that school does not need to be the same as it was one hundred years ago. We are watching in real time as our outdated education system reaches its breaking point. As it breaks, we see more and more innovation and solutions, with people everywhere trying new things, failing, adapting, and trying again. As parents, we now know what learning looks like outside of a school building—and it is opening our eyes in profound ways. Together, we have an incredible opportunity to apply our learnings to the future of education. In the process, we can revitalize how our children think about school, renew their love of learning, and reignite their pilot lights.

As we face this historic moment together, I have a unique perspective that can help. Four years ago, I had the opportunity to educate my three children outside of the school system.

SCHOOLING OUTSIDE THE SYSTEM

When the pandemic hit, I—like most of us—was worried about COVID-19. But when it came to the disruption of my children's education, I was on familiar ground. Why? In 2016, my family and I made a big decision: to homeschool for one year.

Of course, making a deliberate choice is different than being forcefully disrupted by a global pandemic. Still, the experience of educating my children outside of a conventional school system left us all more confident, better prepared, and quicker to adapt to change.

Looking back, I see that pulling our children out of school was a gutsy move and a big leap that forever changed our lives. My husband calls it our "educational sabbatical." I call it our "year of homeschooling." By either name, our family's yearlong break from school transformed the way we think about and approach education. Most importantly, it rekindled our children's joy of learning—a joy that has sustained them through the challenges and uncertainties of school during the pandemic.

WHERE DID THE LOVE OF LEARNING GO?

The decision to homeschool wasn't a quick one; it was many years in the making. I had become dissatisfied with my children's schooling. I noticed their love of learning dwindling—a feeling many parents can relate to after watching their children struggle through distance and hybrid learning.

My oldest son was finishing sixth grade at the time, and his curiosity was being squelched in favor of doing what was needed to please his teachers. He is bright, inquisitive, and wise beyond his years, and it saddened me to hear him repeat over and over that school was boring.

I studied his school curriculum closely, and it struck me that it was decades old. Contextual information and learning examples were from prior generations and lacked relevance. Endless worksheets did little to ignite his curiosity or imagination, and there were few hands-on opportunities to make his learning come alive. Based on twenty-first-century standards, my son was right: school was boring.

He was quick to learn that a "good student" sits quietly, listens attentively, and follows instructions—even though he prefers to learn by collaborating with others. His teachers rewarded "correct" answers, so he saved his deeper questions for home. I rationalized my doubts and silenced my intuition, but it was plain to see that my son was losing interest in school.

IS YOUR CHILD LOSING INTEREST IN SCHOOL?

Mark which are true for your child and which are false.

My child was an engaged and happy learner, but something changed.	☐ True ☐ False
My child questions the value, importance, or relevance of what is taught.	☐ True ☐ False

My child is curious at home but does not show curiosity in schoolwork.	☐ True	☐ False
My child is creative at home but does not show creativity in schoolwork.	☐ True	☐ False
My child believes grades, test scores, and teacher approval determine their worth.	☐ True	☐ False
My child tells me they are stressed out by school, tests, grades, and homework.	☐ True	☐ False
My child lacks motivation to do homework or does the minimum to get it done.	☐ True	☐ False
My child's homework interferes with family time, downtime, playtime, or sleep.	☐ True	☐ False
My child's schoolwork constrains their ability to build upon their unique strengths.	☐ True	☐ False
My child is afraid of making mistakes or asking questions at school.	☐ True	☐ False
My child's focus is on studying instead of on learning.	☐ True	☐ False
My child does not want to read for school but enjoys reading at home.	☐ True	☐ False
My child feels like they already know what is being taught.	☐ True	☐ False
My child does not talk about school or schoolwork in a positive way.	☐ True	☐ False
My child has stopped expressing a desire to learn or read about anything.	☐ True	☐ False

If you answered *true* to several questions, your child might be losing interest in school.

While it was evident that my son was bored, at home his focus shifted to personal passions, interests, and curiosities. He devoured the *Harry Potter* books and learned everything he could about hockey and fishing. He was curious about new and emerging technologies such as virtual reality, 3-D printing, motion graphics, and editing. So why was his love of learning so stifled at school?

My middle son was also stagnating in his fourth-grade classroom. Later I would learn about the fourth-grade slump in my master's program at Drexel University's School of Education. The slump is a well-documented decline in school enthusiasm often attributed to a greater focus on testing and achievement instead of natural curiosity and love of learning. Many parents describe the slump as an abrupt and worrisome dislike of school.

My son definitely entered the slump. Throughout his schooling, he demonstrated an ability to learn new concepts quickly and with enthusiasm. He skipped a grade, which kept him challenged until he landed in an inflexible classroom that left no room for creativity and autonomy. While many parents relate to this feeling, we tolerate it and tell ourselves, *it's just a part of school.*

Also, like most fourth graders, my son was expected to complete a stack of homework worksheets every evening. Like many parents, I told myself, *homework is just a part of life; it's building a strong work ethic.* But in my heart, I knew that my eight-year-old's precious free time at home was wasted on busywork that did not advance his learning.

My youngest son had just started preschool at the time. He was still filled with curiosity and questions. One day, he was playing school with a neighbor. She set up a little desk and chair and stood in front of him with a chalkboard. She gave him pretend lessons and praised him when he worked quietly without disrupting the stuffed animal students. She made multiple-choice tests and gave him big stars for correct answers and red marks for mistakes. If any of the stuffed animals "misbehaved," she wrote pink slips for detention. I watched them play and thought, *Is this what learning looks like?* I felt an irrational need to protect his love of learning. I announced, "Recess!" and sent them to play outside.

LOOKING FOR A BETTER WAY

Like the millions of parents who are frustrated with distance learning, I felt frustrated with my children's school experience. I knew there must be a better way for children to learn. As the quote reads at the start of this chapter: "Education is not the filling of a pail, but the lighting of a fire."

To light that fire, children must explore their curiosities, think freely, and ask deep and thought-provoking questions with nonobvious answers. Instead of doing more worksheets, they yearn to discover their own talents, interests, and passions. To break the misconception that learning only happens sitting inside at a desk, let's give them a chance to put down their pencils and lift their eyes to the enormity of their world. This includes spending

Our children deserve to learn heads-up and hands-on—designing, building, testing, failing, and learning to try again.

more time outdoors, climbing trees, building forts, and exploring nature. Our children deserve to learn heads-up and hands-on— designing, building, testing, failing, and learning to try again.

Above all, we want our children to rediscover the joy of learning. Correct answers on a bubble sheet should not define success in school. Instead of fact-memorizers, our world needs problem-finders and problem-solvers who use questions and creativity to find solutions to our world's new and emerging challenges.

Is this vision idealistic compared to the status-quo of school? As I watched my own children move through grade levels, homework increased, free time declined, and assignments became more heads-down. They approached their work with less critical thinking and imagination. Perhaps you have seen this in your children, or in children you know. So many of us ask ourselves, *What can be done?*

Like many parents, I resonated with the late Ken Robinson's TED Talk called "Do Schools Kill Creativity?" Deep down, I knew that our children's creativity wasn't dead; it was just dormant at school. I saw my own children's pent-up creativity manifest at home in fascinating ways, like elaborate backyard games, playful imaginary worlds, improvisational music and song, and plenty of pickup sports games on the neighborhood blacktop.

As a bright spot outside of school, we found creative expression in an extracurricular activity called Odyssey of the Mind.[1] Any school, home school, or community group can join this open-ended problem-solving competition. Teams of up to seven kids work together over many months to solve a problem and build a solution using low or no-cost recycled and repurposed materials. Children of all ages participate, representing all areas of the United States and countries across the world. I coached many teams over the years, taking dozens of kids to the world finals and building relationships with parents, children, and educators worldwide. Through heartfelt conversations, I realized that people everywhere are united in searching for a better way to learn.

SPARKS OF CREATIVITY IN THE CLASSROOM

As the cofounder of a creative agency, I have two decades of experience bringing creative problem-solving into the corporate world. I wondered how I could translate this experience to help kids and teachers in schools. This led to a new chapter in my journey with a program called Kiddovate.

I partnered with an inspired educator named Day Halsey. Together, we developed a creative-thinking tool kit for students and teachers and taught countless workshops in and out of schools. We created booklets, videos, tools, and a mobile app to help classrooms and maker spaces across the United States. We shared our programs at SXSW EDU and the International Society for Technology in Education's largest teacher conference. We met thousands of people working to improve our outdated education system, including large companies and nonprofits. We followed education entrepreneurs disrupting the system, like Elon Musk's Global Learning XPRIZE, which offered fifteen million dollars to the best open-source software empowering children to *teach themselves* basic reading, writing, and arithmetic.

Our Kiddovate programs gained momentum, and many children came to our workshops more than once. While we felt validated by the parents, teachers, and children experiencing our programs, our work wasn't making it into the classroom. Despite our best outreach efforts, teachers were not adopting our successful programs inside of school buildings.

Why? We held focus groups and asked teachers this question. Their honest answers disheartened us. Teachers didn't have time to try new things. They wanted to bring innovative approaches into their classrooms, but teaching the scope and sequence and preparing for standardized tests stretched them too thin. We were advised to think of our program as enrichment that would survive better *outside school.*

OUR FAMILY DISRUPTION

Outside school is where my family landed when fate brought us big news. Our company was starting a project on the West Coast that required both my husband and I to spend more time in California. We evaluated how this travel would impact our family life and agreed that separating for long periods of time was out of the question.

I had been dreaming of homeschooling the children for so long, and this was our chance! I raised the idea of pulling them out of school.

While the children were excited, my husband was skeptical. From my perspective, this was the perfect opportunity to disrupt the status quo, explore a better way, allow them to follow their passions and curiosities, and just plain see what learning could look like outside of school. My husband finally agreed that we could homeschool for just one year, adding: "Even if it's a total flop, we can't mess them up too much in twelve months!"

THE SEVEN WONDERS OF LEARNING

When the pandemic forced school closures, parents suddenly found themselves playing an active role in their children's instruction. Many thought, *Wait, I have no idea how to do this! I'm not a teacher!* I felt that way, too, when I started homeschooling. As the days and weeks of homeschooling unfolded, I asked myself many of the same questions that parents are asking today.

HAVE YOU ASKED YOURSELF THESE QUESTIONS?

- What does learning look like outside of a school building?
- Will online learning work for my child?
- How involved do I need to be in my child's learning?
- How do I know if my child is appropriately challenged?
- How do I keep my child engaged and motivated?
- Is my child making sufficient academic progress? Will my child fall behind?
- How can I support my child's social-emotional well-being?
- How should I structure my child's time? Should I create a schedule and stick to it?
- I do not consider myself good at math; can I still teach math to my child?
- How should I manage my child's screen time?
- How can I keep my child on-task?
- What if my child gets bored?
- Without peers in a classroom, will my child become antisocial?
- How can I personalize my child's learning?

In chapter 1, I will share how our family navigated these questions, and many more, and discovered what I now call the Seven Wonders of Learning.

Throughout our homeschool year, our family embraced a new paradigm. We learned, unlearned, and relearned. We redefined how we used our time. We unlocked curiosity and embraced hands-on, experiential learning through making and doing. We unleashed creativity and rediscovered our individuality. And throughout the journey, we rekindled the joy of learning.

I hope these Seven Wonders of Learning will help your family better navigate school outside the status quo as they helped ours.

Like the Seven Wonders of the Ancient World, they have stood the test of time. I am not the first—and I won't be the last—to espouse the values of unlearning, free time, curiosity, hands-on experiences, creativity, individuality, and joy. From Ancient Rome to Silicon Valley to the laboratories where scientists are developing innovative treatments and vaccines, these tenets are at the heart of true learning and discovery.

LIGHTING THE TORCH

My family has carried the torch of these Wonders since our home-school year, and your family can, too. They lit the way as my children returned to school after our homeschooling year, and they do so still today as they adapt to different modes of learning during the disruption of school. These core tenets also light the way as I homeschool my youngest son during the pandemic.

Now I would like to pass the torch to you. I hope this book helps you revitalize, reimagine, and transform how you think about school and learning—during the pandemic and beyond. Whether your child is experiencing online or hybrid public or private school, homeschool or a learning pod, or something else new or different, I hope the Wonders in this book will make that experience more engaging and meaning-ful. After reading this book, I hope you have a new perspective that empowers you to take steps to revitalize your child's school experience for the better—on your own terms, with your own children, starting today.

In the end, after this wild roller-coaster ride of school disruption is over, I believe we will look back at 2020 and realize that it triggered an important period of growth, adaptation, and innovation that gives us a clear, new vision for a better way to learn.

UNLEARNING

*The illiterate of the 21st century will not be
those who cannot read and write, but those
who cannot learn, unlearn, and relearn.*

—ALVIN TOFFLER

SCHOOL, DISRUPTED

After the COVID-19 pandemic hit, the scope and speed of school closures was unprecedented. As of March 30, 2020, UNESCO estimated that 87 percent of the world's students—1.5 billion learners in 180 countries—were affected. These numbers grew as the pandemic spread, and by mid-April, 192 countries closed all schools and universities, affecting almost 1.6 billion students.[2,3] Meanwhile, a study completed by Bellwether Education Partners in October 2020 found that up to three million children in the United States have been without any form of education since their schools closed in March.[4]

To put this in context, during the 1918 Spanish flu pandemic, the majority of US cities temporarily closed schools for up to four months, but some only closed for a matter of weeks, and three major metropolises—New York, Chicago, and New Haven, Connecticut—didn't close schools at all.[5]

A school disruption of this scale triggered a roller coaster of change for children, parents, and teachers. If you felt like you were (and still are) on a wild ride, you are right. The image below visualizes the Disruption-Unlearning Curve we experienced as we adapted to the cancellation of schools. Similar to the five stages of grief outlined by Elisabeth Kübler-Ross, this is a process of acceptance and transformation. While not everyone will experience the Disruption-Unlearning Curve in the same way, the same order, or at the same speed, it illustrates how our first Wonder, unlearning, was quietly happening in the background.

THE DISRUPTION-UNLEARNING CURVE

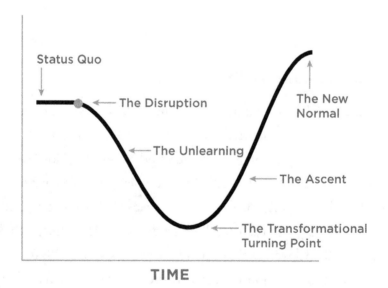

Status Quo

The Disruption

The Unlearning

The New Normal

The Ascent

The Transformational Turning Point

TIME

THE WILD RIDE

The Status Quo

The left side of the image shows life as we knew it with the status quo of schooling. Throughout our entire lives, we depended on our children going to school just as sure as we counted on the sun rising each morning.

The Disruption

Then—*bang!* In a matter of days, schools were closed. The predictability of the status quo abruptly stopped. We felt trapped on a roller-coaster ride we didn't sign up for as we were instructed to buckle up and prepare for the worst. This sudden and overwhelming change sent many of us into shock, denial, and dread. We thought, *this cannot be happening; I don't believe it!* As we struggled to grasp this turn of events and panicked at our unpreparedness, the roller coaster left the station.

The Unlearning

Our lives were destabilized. Many were gripped by a sinking feeling as the world descended into chaos and uncertainty. Our lives turned upside down as we tried to adjust to lockdown, isolation, distance learning, and remote working. How we longed to go back to the status quo! Many of us resisted change and held out hope that *things will go back to normal soon.*

Many of us felt anxious and overwhelmed. We were on pins and needles about furloughs and job cuts. We saw the supply chain come to a halt and experienced shortages in our grocery stores. We saw sickness, hospitalization, intubations, and death—all while grappling with supporting our children's academic, social, and emotional well-being, managing our escalating fears, and keeping a paycheck.

Let's be honest: the first thirty days of lockdown were rough. The laundry piled up. We ate rice and pasta and frozen vegetables. We stopped seeing friends and family, we stopped going to the grocery store, and we even stopped getting out of our pajamas. The goal was simply to survive this "temporary" lockdown to flatten the curve. And we held on, white-knuckled, waiting for the day children would be back in school and life would return to normal.

The Transformational Turning Point

Then, reality began to sink in. For some of us, a sudden turn shifted our perspectives. For others, it was a gradual realization that things were not normalizing. For many of us, this transformation is still happening as we come to accept that there is no going back to the status quo—not now, not soon, and maybe not ever. COVID-19 is here to stay. To move forward and thrive, we have no choice but to accept, adapt, and change our perspectives to embrace a new way of thinking about school.

The Ascent

When the turning point hits, the energy changes. Suddenly, things start to feel possible. Gradually, we can shift focus away from how things used to be and start thinking about how to make things better going forward. Our attachment to the status quo loosens its grip and we become more open to new ideas to improve the school experience for our children.

It's OK if you don't feel this sense of optimism yet. Many parents are still struggling with the seeming impossibility of this situation. With the guidance in this book, I hope to help you and your family tap into the potential that this disruption brings.

The New Normal

We emerge from the wild ride into the "new normal" and wonder, *Is this the new status quo?* It is our instinct to try to restabilize. We may be in store for more twists and turns, but we are becoming better at navigating the disruption of school because we are more aware, adaptable, and open to change.

THE WONDER OF UNLEARNING

Although this ride was (and is) tumultuous and downright scary, did you realize that the process of unlearning was happening the whole time? Unlearning has a few steps. First, we come face-to-face with a belief system that is no longer working. Second, we replace the outdated beliefs with a new way of thinking that could work better. Finally, we try to rebuild day-to-day life around the new mindset.

During the lockdown, we had to unlearn the way we had attended school for generations. As the saying goes, we let go of the old to make way for the new. Then we began to slowly adapt and search for a new model to get us through the pandemic.

Our children were forced to rapidly unlearn the status quo. Everything they valued was stripped away: no school, no sports, no visits with friends, no parties, no graduations, no contact. When schools closed and scrambled to implement online classes, students were forced to learn in a completely different way for which they had no existing mental model. The routine they habitually followed every school day for years was upended.

Now, isolated in their homes in a worldwide pandemic, they were expected to wake up, log in to a digital learning platform, like Zoom or Google Meet, and "go to school." But nothing about distance learning was familiar. They could not sit face-to-face with peers or teachers. They could not learn in a typical classroom. They could not raise their hands in the same way.

WHAT HAS YOUR CHILD NEEDED TO UNLEARN?

The following are just a few examples shared by students of various ages when asked, "What have you had to unlearn?"

- "Starting the day together in morning circle."
- "Walking to the corner to wait for the bus with my friends."
- "Dropping in to see my teachers for help during study hall."
- "Playing kickball on the playground."
- "Turning my homework in on the bin on my teacher's desk."
- "Working on group projects together in the library."
- "Joking around in the hallway for a few minutes between classes."
- "Taking turns changing the calendar and weather board."
- "Greeting my principal each morning with a handshake."
- "Looking around my classroom to see who is absent."
- "Going on field trips to fun places."
- "Clowning around in the locker room."
- "Hanging out with my friends and trading food during lunch."
- "Caring how I look when I go to school."

Parents also experienced rapid unlearning. For years, we attended school. Then, we sent our children to school. (We have double the amount of old-school thinking as our children!) Suddenly, there was no more getting them ready for school, packing lunches or backpacks, or shuttling them around before and after school. Instead, we found ourselves spending hours per day supervising our children in distance learning, all while trying to keep our jobs and sanity.

Many teachers went through rapid unlearning as well. At first, some replicated status quo lesson plans in a digital format. Unfortunately, this did not work well, and many students suffered through long, monotonous days in front of computer screens. It's no wonder many of our children grew weary, depressed, irritable, and withdrawn. The most adaptive teachers saw that students were disconnected and disengaged. These teachers began to unlearn how they taught school for their entire careers to find new ways to teach in the pandemic—and bravo to those who led the charge.

Many of us—parents, students, and teachers alike—built our lives on these old-school mental models, and our deeply ingrained beliefs about

Our deeply ingrained beliefs about school were hard to shake off.

school were hard to shake off. As the roller-coaster analogy shows, dropping away from the status quo can be terrifying, especially when we don't know when or how the ride will end. It requires a complete reorientation of thinking.

I learned this challenging lesson during our homeschool year when I hit the wall of my own status quo thinking. Looking back, we experienced a period of rapid unlearning too. And just like today, to move forward, we couldn't ignore it, avoid it, go around it, or jump over it; we had to go *through* it to get to the other side. The experience taught me why unlearning is the most essential of all the Wonders—it unlocks the rest.

STUCK IN THE OLD-SCHOOL MENTAL MODEL

When we pulled our children out of school, we did not think it would prepare them to adjust to a total disruption of the education system. Our homeschooling experience helped them transition to this new learning model because they had been exposed to learning outside the system.

But we didn't get there without needing to unlearn deeply held beliefs about school—the same kind of unlearning parents around the globe are doing now as we face this pandemic.

> **We didn't get there without needing to unlearn deeply held beliefs about school.**

I'll be honest: the first month of homeschooling challenged both my children and me. Starting with the curriculum, there were so many options for "boxed" programs sold by grade level, but they felt too standardized. I wanted our homeschool to be hands-on and experiential, and I felt frustrated by the lack of curriculum emphasizing this type of learning. I decided to build our curriculum à la carte, which took way more time and research than I expected.

Next, we needed a daily routine. On Labor Day weekend, I pushed my Microsoft Excel skills to the edge to create a homeschool schedule. Creating a routine that would work for everyone was an arduous task. Finally, I formulated a color-coded spreadsheet jam-packed with humanities, science, math, free reading, backyard snack, STEM lab, journal writing, nature walk, music, art, trampoline, quiet reflection, playtime, and Friday spelling bee.

The Tuesday after Labor Day, we started school. My children were troupers, but we were overscheduled to the minute. Determined to adhere to my spreadsheet, I tried to keep everything on schedule, even as I fell behind in my own job. I had accounted for the time we would spend learning but underestimated the time I would spend planning. I quickly discovered that homeschooling was a significant time commitment, more than I ever imagined.

We crashed at the end of week three. My husband was out of town, and the boys and I were scheduled to take our Friday field trip, but we were too exhausted. While the big boys zoned out in front of the television and my youngest son napped, I took a much-needed break.

I retreated to my bedroom and had a breakdown. This wasn't fun, exciting, or inspiring. It was a grind. I tossed and turned that night, thinking about how to make things better. *Was this the wrong curriculum? Did we need more multimedia? More time in the day for free play?* Ideas swam through my mind all night. In the morning, I woke with a bright idea: *let's do our field trips on Mondays so the boys do the fun stuff first!*

I Googled "short fun field trips near me" and I found a place called the Historic Seneca Schoolhouse. The website said it was a popular destination for elementary school field trips because children go back in time to experience an authentic nineteenth-century school day. *Perfect!* I thought. This would be a great juxtaposition to our modern-day homeschool, plus it would get us out of the house to do something experiential. I clicked through the site to find the contact information, and a picture caught my eye.

© 2013 Mark Bobb Photography

I must have stared at this historic picture of the Seneca School-house for ten minutes. I imagined my boys sitting at these wooden desks, neatly arranged in rows, while a teacher in a long skirt gave a history lesson at the chalkboard. I imagined them switching between subjects guided by the ticking of a big, round clock—working quietly with their heads down, reading from books, practicing math and handwriting, and studying words for a Friday spelling bee.

I snapped back to reality with an uncomfortable realization: even though the Seneca Schoolhouse was built in the 1800s, it was strikingly similar to *my* modern-day homeschool. My children sat at a table to read and write. When the hour changed, they switched subjects. They consumed content that I selected. The chalk slates had been replaced with notebooks and iPads, but the format was the same, right down to my stinkin' Friday spelling bee. Besides the look and feel of the furniture, the clothing, and maybe a dunce cap hiding in the corner, I had recreated this model of school in my own home.

Sound familiar?

This is exactly what happened with distance learning in the spring of 2020. We got stuck trying to replicate the nineteenth-century school day over Zoom—and it was awful. Recreating the schedule of an in-person school day in an online format was not an effective way for our children to learn. Some would even say this was an abject failure that

> **We got stuck trying to replicate the nineteenth-century school day over Zoom—and it was awful.**

will have long term negative consequences on our children. Children with access to computers monotonously signed into school at 9:00 a.m. every morning, staring bleary-eyed at their screens all day before signing off at the end of the school day. Those without computers or internet connections had even more challenges.

Parents, students, and teachers alike grew weary and disengaged. Clearly, what was happening on Zoom wasn't school. It wasn't learning. *Then what was it?*

It was unlearning.

LOOKING AT LEARNING THROUGH A NEW LENS

The pandemic has led to a society-wide scrutiny of school and learning through the very personal lens of our own children. Lockdown and distance learning have brought parents up close and personal with their children's schooling more than ever before. Under the microscope, we have seen things we've never seen and felt things we've never felt.

We've gotten a bird's-eye view into our children's virtual classrooms, teachers, and curriculum. In some cases, we have seen upbeat teachers taking attendance at 9:00 a.m. sharp. In other cases, we've seen teachers assigning optional worksheets graded only for completion. We have seen some teachers make creative and engaging videos to enliven distance learning, and others present the same old slides for an entire class period. We've seen inconsistency, gaps, and disparity. Some school systems have invited parents to provide feedback on what they see, while others resisted parental involvement. One school district in Tennessee asked parents to sign a contract forbidding them from observing their children's virtual classes.[6]

Many of us worried about some aspects of what we saw and slowly started to lose faith in the school system's ability to meet the challenges of the times. The list below captures some of the things parents have felt during this period of rapid unlearning.

COMMON CONCERNS DURING THE DISRUPTION OF SCHOOL

Mark which are true for you and which are false.

I worry that my child will fall behind.	☐ True	☐ False
My child has too much free time during the day.	☐ True	☐ False
If I'm not supervising distance learning, it won't happen.	☐ True	☐ False
With no supervision, my child will surf the web or play video games all day.	☐ True	☐ False
I worry about how to keep my child motivated and engaged.	☐ True	☐ False
I worry that my child is learning less and retaining nothing.	☐ True	☐ False

I worry that my child's grades and GPA will slip.	☐ True	☐ False
I worry that my child isn't learning any science at all.	☐ True	☐ False
My child needs more help with distance learning, but none is available.	☐ True	☐ False
My child is having a hard time understanding but will not speak up.	☐ True	☐ False
I worry that my child is becoming depressed, withdrawn, and isolated.	☐ True	☐ False
My child hasn't been contacted by a school counselor.	☐ True	☐ False
I have not been contacted by my child's teacher.	☐ True	☐ False
My child is too young to do distance learning all day.	☐ True	☐ False
Our school system is taking so long to adapt.	☐ True	☐ False
We do not have the resources or supplies to help our child stay on track.	☐ True	☐ False
We don't have reliable internet or computer access at home.	☐ True	☐ False
I struggle with supervising remote learning while working from home.	☐ True	☐ False
I feel guilty because I can't help my child when I'm working, yet I can't work when I am helping my child.	☐ True	☐ False
I wake up early to work before my child wakes up.	☐ True	☐ False

I stay up late to work after my child goes to bed.	☐ True	☐ False
I have considered quitting work to help my child with distance learning.	☐ True	☐ False
I have considered private school, homeschool, or other options.	☐ True	☐ False
During the pandemic, it looks like I'm responsible for my child's learning.	☐ True	☐ False

These are new thoughts to many parents. Our society has out-sourced education to schools for generations, so asking these questions reveals a huge shift in thinking. As parents, we begin to answer these questions by unlearning everything we thought we knew about school.

UNLEARNING SCHOOL

Of course, this is easier said than done, as I discovered when I unconsciously recreated a traditional school in my own home. Like it or not, I inherited the nineteenth-century model of thinking about school. Truth be told, we all did. Seneca Schoolhouse is deeply ingrained in most of us.

If you're like most parents and caregivers, the traditional model of education is entrenched in your belief system. Regardless of culture, zip code, gender, socioeconomic status, age, or level of education, you likely believe that children should go to school. From the time they enroll in kindergarten to the time they graduate high school, you expect your children to move through each grade linearly, accumulating knowledge as they do their homework, study for tests, and pursue good grades. You likely believe that better grades mean a better chance of getting into a good college. This is what we were all taught to believe.

When your child studies their subjects, you might laugh and think, *I remember learning that.* Your parents and grandparents probably learned it, too, because the standard scope and sequence have hardly changed for generations. From the first day on the bus to the day of graduation, your child is on the same conveyer belt that you were on, moving with millions of children every year toward their future lives.

Until the conveyer belt abruptly stopped. Then, you peered over their shoulder during distance learning and began to wonder: *Is there a better way?*

WHAT WOULD CHILDHOOD LOOK LIKE WITHOUT SCHOOL AS WE KNOW IT?

Before the pandemic, this question stopped people in their tracks. Now that we are confronted with the reality of a different kind of school and new way of learning, some of us are struggling to grasp it. We find it hard to fathom a childhood that is not anchored by a linear progression through a school system. It is difficult for some of us to imagine how our children could possibly learn outside a school building.

Since the day we were born, we have been conditioned to hold many beliefs simply because they are commonly held. Sometimes this status quo thinking is invisible. We subscribe to popular ways of doing, thinking, and living because they just seem to work. We don't even recognize that there are other ways of doing things because the status quo is all we've ever known.

The pandemic has revealed the status quo of school and exposed the limitations and inflexibility of the system. During lockdown, outside a school building, nineteenth-century learning failed. New types of learning emerged that we explore throughout this book. Many of us are beginning to recognize that school is not always learning, and learning is not always at school. Learning is not always a place, or a curriculum, or students sitting at desks facing a teacher. Learning is not a linear progression of subjects throughout the school day, with a short break for lunch or recess. Learning is so much more than the Seneca Schoolhouse model.

The Wonder of unlearning school at home during the pandemic has taught us that our children do not need to depend on a nine-teenth-century classroom to learn. As of the end of 2020, the vast majority of students in the United States were still in virtual-only or hybrid learning environments[7]—yet learning is still happening every-where in new and unexpected ways. Learning has no walls. It is a lifelong experience, built on a nonlinear flow of knowledge that happens anytime, anywhere, with anyone, in structured and unstruc-tured ways.

> ## School in a *place* is only one way to get an education.

School in a *place* is only one way to get an education.

As a parent, it's time to shift focus from school to *learning*. That shift in focus, that shift in thinking, is what will enable us—parents, teachers, and students—to educate our children suc-cessfully now and for years to come. By shifting focus from school to learning, we can help our children rediscover the joy of learning in this pandemic-stricken world, and beyond.

A NEW WAY TO LEARN

After my revelation about the Seneca Schoolhouse, it was suddenly clear why the first three weeks of homeschool had not been successful. It had nothing to do with curriculum, field trips, or more free time;

rather, it had everything to do with an outdated mental model. We needed a new mental model, and fast.

I threw out the color-coded spreadsheet, and we spent the next week exploring the history of school. We learned that during an earlier time in history, standardized schooling protected children from bad working conditions and set a new vision for a better-educated American workforce. After more than a hundred years of this model, my kids and I agreed that standardized education was now stale, outdated, and needed reinvention.

That was when things started to get fun. I asked the boys to brainstorm what was missing from standardized education, and they gave these answers, in no particular order: games, creativity, talking at lunch, exploration, electronics, fishing, curiosity, independence, personalization, fun, laughter, movement, play, variety, family, teams, making things, different languages, music, sports, motivation, relevance, innovation, debate, free time, mistakes, friendships, goals, risk-taking, technology, uniqueness, ideas, feedback, surprises, comfortable clothes, health, excitement, and love.

While our minds were open, I wanted to explore all of our assumptions about school. I wondered if my husband and I held onto deeper-seated beliefs than the boys, and if we could work together to sleuth them out and reverse them. To find out, we came up with the idea of Reverse Day.

We woke up and ate dinner for breakfast. We wore our clothes backward and put our shoes on the wrong feet. We put up extra-large sticky notes along the walls, and listed all the things we associate with school. We circled the most prominent assumptions on our wall stickies, and then we intentionally tried to reverse them.

As we playfully worked through our assumptions, we laughed, imagined, and re-visioned what school could be. New ideas and opportunities began to emerge, and we started to get excited. By letting go of what we believed to be true, we began to make room for something better. Below is an excerpt from our list of reversals.

REVERSING STATUS QUO ASSUMPTIONS ABOUT SCHOOL

ASSUMPTION	REVERSAL
School is required.	School is optional; learning is required.
School is a daytime activity.	Learning is an anytime activity.
School is a place outside the home.	Learning is anyplace.
The same ages learn the same things.	Kids of all ages have learning choices.
Creativity is only for art class.	Creativity belongs in every subject.
Kids do homework at home.	Home is for family and fun.
School is about getting the right answers.	Learning is about asking the right questions.
School is measured by tests.	Learning is measured by curiosity.
School is sitting down and doing worksheets.	Learning is getting up and doing and making.
At school, teachers tell kids what to learn.	Learning gives kids a voice in what they want to learn.
A school day is structured to the minute.	Learning prioritizes unstructured free time.

DISTINGUISHING SCHOOL FROM LEARNING

A new mindset emerged through this process. We felt invigorated. We were asking questions, having conversations, and making progress toward defining a new way of thinking about school.

In the spirit of curiosity, I woke up the next day and wrote a bold question on a big wall sticky: *What would make homeschool wondrous?*

The only rule was that we had to answer the question with a question. The children asked questions that led to more questions, and we documented them all. Over a few days, I wrote down more than one hundred questions about school.

Through these questions, we created a vision for our homeschool. We wanted a place where we could unlearn limiting beliefs, enjoy free and unstructured time, tap into our own curiosity, take field trips, make and build things, be creative, and just be ourselves as we unleashed the joy of learning.

SCHOOL, REBORN

Something wonderful happened: our house became a learning house—all the time. Curiosity was not confined to a fixed number of hours in a school day. Nor was learning limited to a specific place. We were always learning, everywhere, all the time.

The boys read challenging fiction that they chose for themselves. They wrote beautiful papers, and revised them often, as they thought of new ways to make them better. They personalized their history classes based on their own curiosities, choosing to study topics like the history of music, the history of flight, the history of dystopian fiction, and the history of comics. They learned to cook dinner, bake, and barbecue. They learned several different problem-solving approaches available for free online, such as the OODA loop, George Polya's problem-solving process, and the design thinking model created by IDEO and the Stanford d.school. They built robots, CO_2 cars, and giant catapults. They learned how to write code using Scratch, made their own video games, and learned Adobe After Effects, Premiere, and Photoshop. They got CPR certified and earned licenses for boating and hunting. Even during the pandemic, many similar activities are available online. I will talk more about exciting virtual field trips in chapter 4.

Over the year of homeschooling, the children's education was relevant, personalized, self-designed, and a constant work in progress. Best of all, they were engaged, challenged, and motivated to learn. It was contagious and transformed our whole house.

Did they fall behind? No. They advanced faster than ever, especially in math, English, and Spanish. They became more self-driven in their studies, and it showed in their writing, organization, and confidence. They connected with their personal creativity and explored outlets for creative expression.

Did they become awkward and unsocialized? No. They kept alive their close friendships and started new ones with different people of all ages outside their school groups.

Did they sit around all day and play on electronics? No. They played sports, competed in Odyssey of the Mind, played outside, and actually had time to get to know themselves.

Were our days haphazardly scheduled with absolutely no structure? Not at all. A flexible daily routine emerged that was tailored to each child. Focused periods of learning alternated between periods of joyful free time. Before our family experienced learning outside the system, it was hard to imagine how a nontraditional school day would look and feel. Now, because of the global disruption of school, families everywhere are starting to imagine new possibilities of their own.

NAVIGATING DISRUPTION

Our family's schooling disruption did not take place in the middle of a pandemic, and today there are added complexities, such as technological difficulties, social and travel restrictions, and health concerns. As parents open their minds to new mental models of schooling, different options are emerging.

Some parents are scared to put their children on a school bus and risk exposure to COVID-19. Families with underlying medical conditions will likely want to keep children home until a vaccine is widely available. These families might be looking for ways to improve online learning, including exploring online public and private schools like K12.com and Connections Academy, which have years of experience teaching kids through an interactive online format.

On the other hand, some parents are scared about *not* sending their kids back to school. For many parents who work outside the home, school closures impact financial stability. These parents might want their local schools to adapt and implement new measures, such as temperature screening, masks, hygiene stations, or even moving classes outdoors.

Others, provoked by this period of rapid unlearning, might be *enjoying* distance learning as they see new possibilities and scenarios in which parents have more choices in what, where, and how their children learn. Thousands of online and social media groups, websites, and blogs are emerging with new schooling possibilities.

Some parents are setting up "learning pods," which are small groups of children gathered together at alternating houses to do schoolwork. This is similar to the co-op model of some preschools, in which parents assist on a rotating basis and participate in the educational program of all the children. A whole new industry is springing up around the learning pod trend as new organizations facilitate connections between pods and teachers or tutors. In some cases, public and private school teachers who do not want to return to the traditional classroom are teaching learning pods instead.

Some families are sharing resources in other ways. For example, a parent with musical skills might teach music to a group of children, while a parent who is strong at math might assist children with math instruction and homework. This is one way that parents are sharing the burden of supervising home instruction while also teaching the "specials" that have been canceled while schools are closed for in-person learning.

There is also a huge surge in supplemental ad-hoc online classes for kids, which gives them one-on-one access to "microteachers" on platforms like Outschool.com—something we'll talk more about in chapter 4.

Other parents are withdrawing their children from school entirely and homeschooling with learning materials they find on their own. Across all states, more parents than ever are inquiring about how to legally homeschool their children, as they seek more stability during this time of unpredictability. Many parents, myself included, are making different choices for different children in the same household. For example, my older boys are still enrolled in school and participating in online and hybrid learning, while my youngest son is homeschooled.

If you're homeschooling or thinking about homeschooling, see Appendix I for a list of some of my favorite homeschooling resources.

We have been forced into a new way of schooling, and parents are making decisions they never thought they would make. Some are forced to leave the workforce to supervise their children's online learning or have decided to homeschool out of necessity. Some have called upon family and community members to offer support. Many have accepted that their children's educations will suffer this year, yet they have no other choice. These are all factors in our collective unlearning and underscore the fact that we are in the midst of a real-time tipping point that is shaping the future of education.

It's hard to grasp the magnitude of a major societal shift while it's happening. The epic disruption of school is changing us profoundly in ways that are not yet fully understood.

Many predict that this rapid disruption will change the way we live, work, learn, and socialize for years to come.

> **The epic disruption of school is changing us in ways that are not yet fully understood.**

It is changing us in ways we have not yet realized, altering our habits, norms, and expectations. For parents, teachers, and students, school will be forever changed.

THE NEW NORMAL

In April and May of 2020, many school systems announced permanent closures through the end of the school year. AP and SAT tests were canceled. Some school systems replaced letter grades with pass/fail grading. Colleges waived testing requirements. Graduation and "moving-on" ceremonies were canceled or moved online.

In June of 2020, researchers began to talk about the COVID-19 slide. No, that's not a new dance on TikTok; it's a term education experts use to describe historic academic regression and negative impacts on social and emotional well-being. While there's no precedent in research for this kind of disruption in learning, early studies show that the pandemic will result in historic academic regression. CDC research confirms that the abrupt shift to distance learning negatively impacted academic learning and social and emotional well-being—putting even more pressure on parents to help their children thrive.[8]

Early studies show that the pandemic will result in historic academic regression.

Back in March, a neighborhood friend burst into tears when she got word that preschools were closing through the end of the school year. As a lawyer, she was juggling three rambunctious children while working from home. Realizing that COVID-19 was here to stay and schools were closed indefinitely, she, like many others, realized she would need to create proper learning spaces for her children. Toilet paper was back in stock, but desks and task chairs sold out on Amazon as we began to imagine more permanent work-at-home spaces for our families.

Amid this, my son became a quaran-teen. We tried to have a Zoom party to celebrate his thirteenth birthday, but it just wasn't the same. Weeks of stay-at-home orders took their toll. Like many parents, I began to worry about what lockdown was doing to my children's social and emotional well-being.

The academic year ended with a collective sigh of relief as we reminded ourselves that these "quarantine children" would be the most resilient generation. We entered a Zoom-less summer and carefully eased our children back into limited social interaction.

WHAT NOW?

In early summer of 2020, I stood on the driveway with a group of friends reflecting on all we had learned and unlearned. As we watched our kids ride bikes and scooters, we collectively grappled with the idea that it might be unsafe, or impossible, to send our children back to school in the fall. We worried about our children's learning outcomes and feared they would fall behind with a long-term distance learning model.

Since reopening schools was unlikely, we hoped that school leaders would use summer break to develop a better way to train teachers and improve distance learning, but we wondered if it would actually be any better. Would teachers continue replicating an in-person school day? Would our children fall behind? Should we make a pod? Should we team up and homeschool? What was the best way for our children to learn through this disruption? Would our children be stuck at the computer all day? Should we be rethinking how they spend their time?

As the pandemic continues, this last question is an important one. This rapid period of unlearning has focused our attention on our next Wonder: free time.

KEY TAKEAWAYS

- The unprecedented global disruption of school is an urgent opportunity for parents, students, and teachers to break free from nineteenth-century thinking and reinvent school.

- The nineteenth-century model of learning, symbolized by the historic Seneca Schoolhouse, is deeply ingrained in our collective belief system.

- During the early days of lockdown, students, parents, and teachers were forced to move away from the status quo and *unlearn* deeply entrenched beliefs about school.

- *Unlearning*, first of the Seven Wonders of Learning, has a few basic steps: 1) identify a belief system that is no longer working, 2) replace the outdated beliefs with a new way of thinking that works better, 3) rebuild day-to-day life around the new mindset.

- *Unlearning* resulted in a dramatic increase in new approaches to educating children, such as distance and hybrid learning, pods, co-ops, private teachers, microteachers, and homeschools.

- The pandemic teaches us that our children do not need to be inside a school building to learn. School in a *place* is only one way to get an education.

WHAT NEXT? FIVE WAYS TO BRING
THIS CHAPTER TO LIFE

- **Think:** Reflect on the differences between school and learning in your own life and in your children's prepandemic lives. Now think about the differences between school and learning during the pandemic. What observations can you make?

- **Feel:** Take another look at the Disruption-Unlearning Curve. How did you feel after school was abruptly canceled? How did your children feel? What emotions did your family have during the period of rapid unlearning? Do you remember a transformational turning point in which you realized that you needed to adapt to a new mindset? Describe this moment. Did your children experience a turning point? What emotions did it bring up?

- **Do:** Draw a two-column chart on piece of paper. Label one side "School" and one side "Learning." Take some time to write down your beliefs about school and your beliefs about learning. Are they the same or different? Where do these beliefs come from? Ask your children, and others in your household, to do the same activity. Circle three things that will bring more learning into your child's life today.

- **Act:** Pick up the phone and call a friend who has children. Ask each other to share three things that are missing from your child's current schooling situation. Brainstorm ideas about what you can safely do together that will help your children learn in a better way. For example: Can you start a pod? Share an online class? Take the kids on a virtual field trip? Have a movie night or a book club? Be creative and try something new.

- **Discuss:** Next time you are with a small group of family or friends, in person or on Zoom, ask them to share their perspectives on the future of school. Discuss ways in which disruption caused by the pandemic might open new possibilities for better learning. For example, you might ask: Do you think school will ever return to normal? Do you think virtual school as an option is here to stay? Do you think that hybrid learning is here to stay? Also ask the group to think about any positive things that have resulted from the school disruption.

PERSONAL CHECK-IN: WHAT ARE YOU THINKING?

- What have I unlearned this year?

- What are my outdated beliefs about school?

- What can I do to let go of my beliefs that are no longer working and replace them with a new mental model?

- What is one new thing I can try today to improve my child's learning?

- How do I see the future of school postpandemic?

FREE TIME

*There's never enough time to do
all the nothing you want.*

—CALVIN, *CALVIN AND HOBBES*

THE OVERSCHEDULED GENERATION

Think back to life before the pandemic. What did your family's daily schedule look like? If you are like most parents, I bet your life felt overscheduled, busy, and a little frantic as you moved from activity to activity while longing for a few moments of downtime.

Your child's days were probably chock-full of "enriching" extracurricular activities and appointments, with something on the schedule every afternoon and weekend. Just think of the amount of time you spent driving them between activities—be they gymnastics, piano, tutoring, or visits to the orthodontist.

My prepandemic days started early, preparing breakfast and packing lunches while signing permission slips and searching for shoes hidden by the dog. After school, backpacks were exchanged for hockey bags. The boys barely had time for a snack before I started driving them back and forth to ice rinks and activities. We got home just in time for dinner, homework, and eventually, bedtime. The weekends were just as crazy, packed with games, birthday parties, and sleepovers.

My high schooler was particularly busy, juggling a rigorous schedule with more honors and Advanced Placement classes than our generation knew existed. On top of two or more hours of homework per night, he was overloaded with varsity sports and travel teams, studying for the SAT and AP exams, and participating in extracurriculars. He longed for more downtime with his friends and family, but there was little time left over for fun and relaxation.

Our generation was not this busy, were we? In fact, we weren't.

THE FORGOTTEN WONDER OF FREE TIME

Sociologists Sandra Hofferth and John Sandberg of the University of Michigan compared how children ages three to twelve spent their time between 1981 and 1997 and found that children's free time declined by the equivalent of a full school day per week—7.5 hours. Participation in sports rose 35 percent, and participation in the arts rose 145 percent.[9] Hofferth continued the study in 2013 and found that children's free time dropped an additional 4 percent, and outdoor free time fell by a whopping 50 percent.[10]

But our busy kids love all their activities, right?

Wrong. A study published in 2011 asked 882 girls and boys ages nine to thirteen how they felt about their schedules. Ninety percent said they felt stressed because they were too busy. When asked how often they felt stressed, of that 90 percent, half said they felt stressed once in a while or part of the time, 17 percent said they felt stressed most of the time, and 24 percent said they felt stressed all the time.

Unsurprisingly, when asked about the amount of free time they had, 78 percent of children wished they had more free time.[11]

So why do we sign them up for so many activities?

As parents, we manage our children's fast and furious lives with good intentions. We believe these activities are good for them, setting them up for lives of achievement and

Ninety percent of children feel stressed when they are too busy. Seventy-eight percent of children wish they had more free time.

happiness. After all, we want to give our children every opportunity to reach their dreams. But with unrelenting schedules, many of our children have no time to dream. They have no time to pursue personal interests or hobbies, play outside, try something new, or just relax and have fun. Sleep deprived and bleary-eyed, our children spin on a hamster wheel and learn that "surviving a busy schedule" is the hallmark of a successful childhood, even at the expense of playtime, downtime, and family time.

TOSSED OFF THE HAMSTER WHEEL

Then *bang*—the pandemic hit. In a matter of days, our children were tossed off the hamster wheel. Our once-packed schedules were suddenly empty, and the status quo came to a shocking and dramatic halt.

COVID-19 lockdowns were introduced. Most states ordered schools to be closed for at least three weeks and urged families to "shelter in place." There was no more commute to school or work— only the commute from the coffee maker to the Zoom screen. Like falling dominoes, sports, clubs, lessons, tutors, dentist appointments, and everything else was canceled. Weekend parties, tournaments, playdates, religious services, and community events—gone. Then came the NBA, the MLB, and the Olympics.

We were left at home, fearful and isolated, with vast, blank expanses of *time*—unlike anything recent generations have experienced. Faced with empty schedules, we felt restless inside. No one could have predicted that sheltering in place with an open schedule would trigger what clinicians call "free time anxiety" in millions of children and parents. After living hyperscheduled lives for so long, we felt pressure to go, go, go and do, do, do. Instead of enriching us, our activities had come to define us—so much so that when we had nothing to do, we felt empty. We were like addicts trying to wean ourselves off the structured "industrial-age" clock running our lives. I am talking about that big round clock that has hung in every classroom for generations—the one you watched expectantly as the second hand slowly ticked toward the dismissal bell.

THE INDUSTRIAL-AGE CLOCK

Did you know we have been operating on this industrial-age clock for more than a hundred years? That clock, and our education system, has roots in the industrial revolution, when the goal of schooling was to prepare children to move away from agriculture into industry—a world in which time was regulated not by the sun and moon, but by the factory whistle and the clock. In his best-selling book *Future Shock*, Alvin Toffler described the industrialization of learning in this way: "The whole idea of assembling masses of students (raw material) to be processed by teachers (workers) in a centrally located school (factory) was a stroke of industrial genius."[12]

At Seneca Schoolhouse, the day began with the ringing of a bell. Children lined up and then moved inside to progress through a structured day of classes divided by subject. I bet you had a similar structure in your elementary, middle, and high school classrooms—I know I did. Our children, just like us, marched through their prepandemic school days regulated by this clock. The bell rings when it's time to move to a new class, and it rings again when it's time to be quiet and sit down. This symbolizes an industrial-age view that school should be punctual and organized with no idle time—just like a well-oiled machine.

Sheltering in place outside of the school building, with no clock directing us to switch activities every hour, we began to experience the second of the Seven Wonders of Learning: unstructured free time.

WAIT! WHAT IS FREE TIME?

You'd think a house full of free time would leave us overjoyed—but no! Be honest: many of us missed the schedules that anchored our lives. Dropping the children off at school, taking the same route to work, emptying backpacks, washing uniforms, and filling water bottles before practice; all these things provided a sense of comfort. I know I missed the mundane things like grabbing an afternoon coffee, talking with a parent at a music lesson, and my weekly trip to the grocery store. We longed for that familiar structure.

So what did we do? We brought the structure of the industrial-age clock into our own homes.

As we discussed in chapter 1, most schools replicated the full 9:00 a.m. to 3:00 p.m. school day on Zoom. The "virtual bell" transitioned children between Zoom rooms based on the same old industrial-age clock, but when the virtual dismissal bell rang, what were we supposed to do with our children? Now *we* were responsible for filling vast chunks of their time that used to be covered by school and extracurricular activities.

There was an explosion of blogs and social media posts about how to fill up your child's time after virtual school. Headlines like "Twenty Virtual After-School Programs to Keep Kids Engaged When the Learning Day is Done" offered a slew of activities to keep kids entertained every hour, on the hour. Social media influencers extolled the benefits of enforcing a consistent schedule amid the chaos. The common theme was "Set a schedule—and stick to it!" It's no wonder we panicked when we saw our children sitting around doing nothing.

HAVE YOU EXPERIENCED THESE THOUGHTS DURING DISTANCE LEARNING?

Mark which are true for you and which are false.

My child is bored; but I don't know what to do about it.	☐ True	☐ False
I feel like a bad parent for letting my child have so much screen time.	☐ True	☐ False
I feel frustrated and annoyed at having to keep my child busy.	☐ True	☐ False
My child is supposed to be busy in class right now—what's happening?	☐ True	☐ False
If I don't keep my child busy, he or she might get depressed.	☐ True	☐ False
Without any social interaction, my child only has me to play with.	☐ True	☐ False
I can't dedicate any more time to distance learning or I will lose my job.	☐ True	☐ False
Why can't the school offer some after-school activities?	☐ True	☐ False

ENTER SCREEN TIME—THE GREAT PACIFIER

During lockdown, many parents (including me) threw up their hands and gave their children unlimited screen time. In all honesty, my rules flew out the door and I even allowed my eight-year-old to play Fortnite with his best friend. In our house, the Xbox became the conduit for "hanging out" with friends, and when the children played video games, I could at least get some work done. It felt like a necessary compromise, but I didn't feel good about offering them up to the "Screenslaver," a character some of you might recall from Disney's *Incredibles 2*.

Those of you who have seen *Incredibles 2* know what I'm talking about. I'll never forget a prepandemic trip to the movies that revealed just how much the constant flow of digital information infiltrated my own life. While the previews played, I gave in to the temptation to answer some work emails, which led to checking my Instagram feed, which led to seeing who responded to my recent Evite, which led to reading the chat on TeamSnap, which led to buying a new mouthguard for my son on Amazon, which led to ordering dog food, which led me to email the vet to schedule an appointment. All during the previews. I laughed when the movie began with a vignette about an evil villain called the "Screenslaver" who hypnotizes people by broadcasting patterns on any available screen. In the movie, prolonged exposure rots people's brains and turns them into slaves of screen time. Talk about dramatic irony.

Obviously, the conversation around limiting screen time is different in a pandemic. Children must be on screens for school, and screens offer the only way for children to interact with friends and family. What else were we to do? In hindsight, research confirms just how massive the spike in screen time was for all ages. Before the pandemic, average screen time for kids clocked in at three hours per day, but screen time in March 2020 jumped to seven to eight hours per day, which is extremely unhealthy for children.[13]

> **Screen time in March 2020 jumped to seven to eight hours per day, which is extremely unhealthy for children.**

I know many parents, like me, tolerated extreme screen time as a temporary survival mechanism and let it slide. Sure, I heard the whisperings of parental instincts telling me to peel them away from the Xbox, but letting the children binge for a few weeks wouldn't harm them because things would "return to normal" soon. But when schools canceled through the end of the school year, many parents knew it was time to bring down the hammer. Many began to limit the amount of time children spent on their devices—ushering in a whole new era of boredom.

SURRENDERING TO WONDROUS BOREDOM

A few days after reintroducing limits on screen time, my children became super bored. Not just your everyday, run-of-the-mill kind of bored. I mean whiny and moaning, *How could you do this to me?* bored. They insisted there was nothing to do and complained about how terrible I was to restrict video games. Then, one afternoon, my older boys came into the kitchen and announced that they were going for a bike ride.

"Together?" I asked incredulously. "Where to?" They shrugged and left.

They dusted the cobwebs from their bikes, and off they went. Two hours and seventeen miles later, they came back fresh-faced and laughing. They traveled some new roads, found a horse farm, and had some good old-fashioned fun. Soon, my youngest son joined them on their rides. They learned to drift and do tricks. A bike jump was built. Now, many months into the pandemic, biking is an everyday thing.

Soon my children had no problem finding things to do with their free time. Before the pandemic, my oldest son played twenty hours of hockey per week. When the pandemic canceled sports, he was left with vast amounts of empty time. Boredom inspired him to convert part of the garage into a gym. He went out there every day to shoot pucks, train, and work out. My middle son used his free time to start writing and releasing songs. My youngest son learned to go grass sledding on a Styrofoam snow sled, climb trees, do cartwheels, Rollerblade, and ride his bike with no hands.

BOREDOM IS THE GOLDEN TICKET

During the homeschool year, we learned about the creative power of boredom. We even turned boredom into a fun game called Boredom Buster Bingo. The idea is so easy that anyone can try it at home.

Simply draw an empty bingo board on a sheet of paper; then fill in the spaces with fun things that your child can do when they get bored. I tried to include activities of different types, including games, art projects, experiments, outdoor activities, chores, exercise, cooking, magic tricks, and music. I also added seasonal and holiday specific ideas for variety. You could include any ideas that appeal to your child.

Then, I hung the Boredom Buster Bingo board on the refrigerator. When boredom struck, I encouraged the boys to do any activity on the board. When complete, each boy wrote their initials on the space to claim it. When either boy got bingo, we had ice cream.

If you're looking for a list of boredom
busters, see Appendix II.

WHEN WAS THE LAST TIME YOU LET YOUR CHILD WALLOW IN BOREDOM?

We are raising a generation of children so accustomed to consuming digital media that they have forgotten how to do nothing. The second they become bored, they feel a strong urge to *fix* their boredom. They reach for their devices to get a quick surge of dopamine by diving into their Minecraft world, playing video games, or checking Snapchat, TikTok, Instagram, or YouTube. The irony is that the more our children silence their boredom with screens, the more they rely on *consumption* because they are literally rewiring their brains to expect constant stimulation.

Trevor Haynes, a research technician in the Department of Neurobiology at Harvard Medical School, summarizes the underlying science of how dopamine-driven feedback loops work and how platforms like Facebook, Snapchat, and Instagram leverage the same neural circuitry used by slot machines and cocaine to keep our kids addicted to their screens.[14]

Haynes says, "Dopamine is a chemical produced by our brains that plays a starring role in motivating behavior. It gets released when we take a bite of delicious food, when we have sex, after we exercise, and, importantly, when we have successful social interactions. In an evolutionary context, it rewards us for beneficial behaviors and motivates us to repeat them."

Every time our children earn digital badges, win a game, or swipe, scroll, tap, or "pull to refresh" whatever feed they check, they get a boost of dopamine in their brain that drives them to do it again, and again, and again. Haynes continues:

> Similar to slot machines, many apps implement a reward pattern optimized to keep you engaged as much as possible. Variable reward schedules were introduced by psychologist B. F. Skinner in the 1930s. In his experiments, he found that mice respond most frequently to reward-associated stimuli when the reward was administered after a varying number of responses, precluding the animal's ability to predict when they would be rewarded. Humans are no different; if we perceive a reward to be delivered at random, and if checking for the reward comes at little cost, we end up checking habitually.

According to Haynes, this is why we, and our children, compulsively check our devices at the slightest feeling of boredom. In fact, the programmers who make the apps and games our children love work very hard behind the scenes to maintain their urge to seek more dopamine rewards.

Haynes cautions:

> Although not as intense as a hit of cocaine, positive social stimuli will similarly result in a release of dopamine, reinforcing whatever behavior preceded it. Cognitive neuroscientists have shown that rewarding social stimuli—laughing faces, positive recognition by our peers, messages from loved ones—activate the same dopaminergic reward pathways. Smartphones have provided us with a virtually unlimited supply of social stimuli, both positive and negative. Every notification, whether it's a text message, a 'like' on Instagram, or a Facebook notification, has the potential to be a positive social stimulus and dopamine influx.

Social media and gaming companies will continue to do everything they can to keep our children's eyes glued to screens. Haynes adds, "And by using algorithms to leverage our dopamine-driven reward circuitry, they stack the cards—and our brains—against us."

As parents, I hope this helps to explain why it is not always easy to prevent screen time from overtaking our children's lives. Addiction to electronics is a real threat for our children. It's no wonder that the World Health Organization (WHO) declared "gaming disorder" as a global health threat in 2019.[15]

Here are ten tips to help avoid filling free time with screen time, and a gentle reminder that parents, too, can model healthy screen time usage by implementing these tips for ourselves.

10 TIPS TO REDUCE SCREEN TIME

1. Disable notifications on your children's devices.

2. Do not keep the television on for background noise.

3. Create "screen time free" areas in your home where electronics are not allowed.

4. Use parental controls to set screen time limits and content restrictions.

5. Consider changing screen time from a daily habit to a privilege that is earned.

6. Agree on a daily screen time limit across all media and use a timer to stay on track.

7. Commit to keeping your child's bedroom a completely screen free room.

8. Choose to eat your meals without any screens at all.

9. Do not allow screen time during car rides—those minutes add up.

10. Take a week long break from screens, and let your children work through the boredom.

When children are bored, they eventually figure out how to generate their own entertainment. They might complain, but they will come up with something to do, whether that means playing checkers or a game of hide-and-seek, skipping rocks, or shooting baskets. By pushing through boredom, children learn to use their imaginations, think inventively, solve their own problems, and express themselves—to *create*, rather than just *consume* (something we'll talk about more in chapter 4).

The pandemic is teaching us to *unlearn* the hamster-wheel lifestyle and stop filling our children's time. We are learning that our overscheduled children often claim there's "nothing to do" because their imaginations have weakened. It's important that we do not jump in to fix or silence their boredom. Only then will we discover that if we do not fill up every second of their lives with activities or screen time, our children will find creative ways to entertain themselves, which is essential to a child's developing brain.

CHILDREN'S DEVELOPING BRAINS NEED FREE TIME

Scientists have found that when we are bored, our brains are not idle. Boredom turns on an important neural network called the default mode network (DMN). The DMN is especially active during introspective activities, such as daydreaming, making sense of the past, and thinking about others. In a review of research for *Perspectives on*

Psychological Science, Mary Helen Immordino-Yang and her coauthors found that the DMN is essential in recalling memories, imagining the future, and feeling social emotions with moral connotations. Neuroscientists now know that free time allows our brains the space to process and develop identity, understanding, and morality.[16]

Scientists also discovered that the DMN is intricately tied to curiosity, creativity, and imagination. To *create* and not *consume,* the mind must occasionally be idle and free to wander, explore, and take new pathways. Idle thinking "is as indispensable to the brain as vitamin D is to the body and, deprived of it, we suffer a mental affliction as disfiguring as rickets," Tim Kreider writes in *The New York Times.* "The space and quiet that idleness provides is a necessary condition for standing back from life and seeing it whole, for making unexpected connections and waiting for the wild summer lightning strikes of inspiration—it is, paradoxically, necessary to getting any work done."[17]

> To *create* and not *consume,* the mind must occasionally be idle and free to wander, explore, and take new pathways.

When children are overscheduled with demanding external activities, homework, and screen time, their default mode networks rarely turn on. In contrast, when children experience free time and boredom, the DMN is busy working in the background, giving their brains much-needed space for reflection—and wondrous things begin to happen. They start to wrestle with unresolved issues and work through emotions that help them make sense of their inner and outer worlds. They ask questions and grapple with problems as part of contemplating their own morality. Alone with their thoughts, they begin to know themselves. They think deeply about their own identity, dreams, and ideas—leading to an increase in creativity and imagination, which we will talk about more specifically in the next chapter.

FREE TIME IS OXYGEN THAT FEEDS THE FIRE

Living through a pandemic has triggered a widespread shift in perspective about how our children spend their time. Could it be that we, as a society, went berserk? Can we look back at our prepandemic lives and see that filling schedules to the brim and piling on homework, tests, and scheduled activities were blocking out any opportunity for free time? Can we see how harmful it was to run like mad from one thing to the next all day, every day? Now we have an incredible opportunity to bring this new perspective of embracing free time into the future of school and learning.

Even when the pandemic eventually lifts and activities return, we don't have to go back to the way things were. Instead, we can protect our children's free time like a watchdog—because we now know that free time is the oxygen that feeds the fires of creativity, individuality, imagination, and joy.

KEY TAKEAWAYS

- In the last several decades, children's free time has declined dramatically.

- When schools closed and our busy schedules abruptly halted, millions of parents and children experienced "free time anxiety."

- It's important to not try to fix or silence children's boredom. They will find ways to entertain themselves.

- The more our children silence boredom with screens, the more they rely on *consumption* and its addictive dopamine rewards in the brain.

- Scientists know that when children are bored, their brains are not idle. Boredom turns on an important neural network called the default mode network (DMN).

- Neuroscientific research proves that free time gives children's brains the space to process and develop identity, understanding, morality, creativity, and imagination, among other vital things.

WHAT NEXT? FIVE WAYS TO BRING THIS CHAPTER TO LIFE

- **Think:** Reflect on your busy prepandemic life. How many of the activities on your family's schedule were chosen by your children? How many were chosen by a parent or caregiver? Think about why each activity was scheduled, and if this activity should be a priority. Is there anything that you would omit in the future to create more free time?

- **Feel:** During the first weeks and months of lockdown, did you or your children experience "free time anxiety?" What feelings did it bring up? List five negative and five positive emotions that you feel about free time. Ask your children and other members of your household to do the same. What do you notice or observe about your feelings after doing this activity?

- **Do:** Check out the boredom busters in Appendix II. Then, add five (or more) additional ideas of your own to build up a list of ideas to try when your kids say they're bored. Challenge your children to add more ideas to the list; then post it on your refrigerator.

- **Act:** Write down a plan for both free time and screen time. First, talk to your child about free time. Do they want more or less? Help them create a plan to achieve their free time goals. Next, discuss screen time. Decide how much of your child's free time can be spent using electronics. Set a clear limit with your child and explain why this limit protects their developing brain.

- **Discuss:** Talk with your children about all their prepandemic activities. Which ones did they enjoy? Which ones felt like chores? Which ones do they really miss and are excited to return to? Which ones can they do without, or replace with something they are more passionate about? Ask your child what they might try if they had more free time.

PERSONAL CHECK-IN: WHAT ARE YOU THINKING?

- During the pandemic, what have I learned about the importance of free time? How can I apply this to my family life?

- Looking back, how has my child's free time been impacted by school, extracurriculars, and optional activities?

- Have my thoughts and feelings changed about my children being bored? If so, how?

- After the pandemic, will I approach my family's schedule in the same way? Why or why not?

- In reflecting on screen time in my family, what might I change moving forward? Are there any aspects of this change that will be harder than others?

CURIOSITY

I think, at a child's birth, if a mother could ask
a fairy godmother to endow it with the most
useful gift, that gift should be curiosity.

—ELEANOR ROOSEVELT

During quarantine, free time led to an explosion of curiosity and questions.

It's interesting to look at Google Trends to compare the questions we asked in spring 2019 versus spring 2020. As the *Washington Post* reported, "In April 2019, Americans wanted to know what a black hole was, who was playing in the Final Four and how many episodes of *Game of Thrones* there were. In April of 2020, we wanted to know how to make masks, how to file for unemployment, and how to find toilet paper."[18]

The year 2020 gave rise to completely new lines of questioning. We watched trusted experts come up short for answers and begin to ask questions instead. For example, when political and medical leaders could not provide decisive answers about COVID-19, they began asking questions: "Why is this disease hurting some people and not others? Is it airborne, spread through droplets, or surfaces? What treatment options do we have while we wait for a vaccine?"

We also saw community leaders asking questions: "Why is it taking so long to get reliable testing? How can we safeguard our vulnerable citizens? How can we deliver food to people in need?"

And we saw our children asking questions too, like: "How do I connect with friends if I can't see them in person? Why does it take so long to make a vaccine? Why do we have to wipe down groceries? And when will I be back in school?"

As parents, we were curious about these things, too, and desperately wanted to have answers. I joked with my friends that if 2020 were a Magic 8-Ball the only answer that would appear through the murky blue liquid again and again is "Cannot predict now."

While 2020 was the year of questions with no decisive answers, there was a silver lining: this was the perfect environment for curiosity to thrive.

THE WONDER OF CURIOSITY

There is a saying that every great invention begins with free time, a question, and the curiosity to pursue it. What led humans to start the first fire, invent the first stone tool, build the first boat, test the first plane? Curiosity. Inventors from ancient history to the modern day have given credit to curiosity for their successes. Thomas Edison said, "I have no special talents, I am only passionately curious."

What is curiosity? Curiosity is an innate spark that drives us to question, explore, discover, experiment, invent, fail, and try again.

It motivates us to seek out new knowledge, learn how things work, and solve problems. When we are curious, we see things differently. We notice detail. We lose track of time. We are less afraid to fail. That's because, as psychologist Todd Kashdan wrote in a 2019 article, curiosity leads us to genuinely want to know more about something, which creates a rare openness to new experiences and the joy of learning.[19]

The wondrous thing is that curiosity requires no special training, only the ability to notice and pursue things we find interesting. With practice, Kashdan notes, curiosity can be called upon in any situation to transform everyday learning into pure joy.

CURIOSITY IGNITES THE JOY OF LEARNING

In Kashdan's book *Curious? Discover the Missing Ingredient to a Fulfilling Life*, he reviews some of the foundational work done on how curiosity produces happiness. He summarizes one of the largest undertakings in the field of psychology in which Martin Seligman, PhD, and Chris Peterson, PhD, devised a scientific classification of basic human strengths. Their research recognized twenty-four strengths that humans can possess, and curiosity was one of the five most highly associated with overall life fulfillment and happiness.[20]

The link between curiosity and happiness shouldn't come as a surprise to parents. We can all think of moments when our children have been compelled to explore something they felt excited about.

> The link between curiosity and happiness shouldn't come as a surprise to parents.

CURIOSITY NATURALLY DRIVES LEARNING WHEN OUR CHILDREN ARE YOUNG

I remember that when my oldest son was five years old, he was fascinated with dinosaurs. What did we do? We took him to the Museum of Natural History to gaze at the giant dinosaur bones. We went to the library and checked out books about dinosaurs. We played backyard games about dinosaurs. We pretended to find dinosaur footprints as we walked around the neighborhood. We chose coloring books and puzzles about dinosaurs. We made dinosaur-shaped cookies.

Imagine all the learning that happened through these experiences. It did not enter our minds to silence his natural curiosity about dinosaurs or force him to be curious about something else. Never did my husband or I say to each other, "Let's convince him to be curious about birds instead." We instinctively knew to support his natural curiosity. But for some reason, when we enroll our children in school, we allow their curiosity to be shifted from what they *want* to learn to what they are *told* to learn. Sometimes, this works out OK because a child is inspired by something in the standard curriculum. But other times, the child's natural curiosity is overlooked and starts to dwindle. During the pandemic, free time gives your child an opportunity to reconnect with their curiosity.

DO SCHOOLS KILL CURIOSITY?

It would be a stretch to say that schools kill curiosity, because many great teachers have the gift of igniting curiosity in our children. But that's the teacher, not the nineteenth-century education system. As parents, we can't expect schools to ignite curiosity in our children—not during a pandemic, not ever. Why? Because the system was not created to provoke and nurture individualized paths of inquiry and problem-solving. The system was created to standardize learning, thereby promoting "correct answers" and grades, which we will talk more about in chapter 5.

Throughout their entire school experience, children are taught to seek the right answer, even though science tells us that asking questions leads to better learning. As cognitive scientist Daniel Willingham notes in his book *Why Don't Students Like School?*, it's the question that stimulates curiosity—being told the correct answer suppresses curiosity before it can even get going.[21] The Wonder of curiosity is what jostles our children out of the traditional "circle the correct choice" mindset and makes way for open-ended questions that are so vital to learning.

WHAT DOES CURIOSITY DO TO THE BRAIN?

More than one hundred years ago, when our education system was instituted, educators did not understand what we do today about the developing brain. Neuroscience has advanced our understanding of the importance of curiosity as it applies to learning and memory. In fact, studies show that curiosity is a big indicator of academic performance, and just as important as intelligence in determining how well students do in school.[22]

In 2014, researchers at the University of California–Davis conducted a study into what happens to the brain when curiosity is sparked. Participants were asked to rate their curiosity about a series of trivia questions and then were given fMRI scans to analyze brain activity while they thought about the questions that particularly aroused their curiosity.

The experiments revealed two extraordinary things. First, curiosity not only helps us learn about and remember things we find intriguing, but it also helps us learn and remember things we don't find interesting.

The researchers found that curiosity primes the brain to receive information—any information, not just information we are interested in. Second, curiosity activates the hippocampus, the area of the brain involved in creating memories—which is also related to reward and pleasure. When we learn about something that piques our curiosity, the reward and pleasure circuit lights up, giving us a kind of natural high.[23] Just as we talked about dopamine rewards and addiction to screens, isn't it wondrous that curiosity naturally releases the same type of dopamine rewards?

> **When we learn about something that piques our curiosity, the reward and pleasure circuit lights up, giving us a kind of natural high.**

I watched curiosity emerge during our homeschool year, but it didn't happen the way I expected. When I moved away from a rigid color-coded class schedule, I committed to the idea that curiosity should take the wheel. With a more relaxed routine, I expected my kids to flip into "curiosity mode." I imagined that I would just sit back and watch the sparks fly. When it didn't happen that way, I thought for sure I could trigger their curiosity—all in one neatly scheduled one-hour meeting at the kitchen table. (Moving past that "old-school" thinking is tough!)

THE TIDY LIST

Early in the homeschool year, I asked my children to join me at the kitchen table and gave each one a special "curiosity journal." I asked them to number the first page from one to ten and write down the ten things they were most curious to learn. I thought it would be easy for them to jot down ten things that got them excited, but they just stared at each other, fidgeting.

"A list?" said my oldest son.

"Yup!" I answered cheerfully. "We're reinventing school, and you decide what you get to learn!"

The boys looked at each other and then at me. "Do we have to do this now?"

My inner alarm bells started to ring as they stared at their blank journals. I could tell they wanted to do what I asked, but they struggled to think of what to write. One was doodling. The other played with the pen cap. I must have made a worried face because they looked at each other again and then asked, "What kind of stuff do you want us to write?"

"Anything you want. Whatever you are curious about!" I said with an encouraging smile.

After a few quiet minutes, they scribbled a few things in their journals. The curiosity was not flowing out of them like I had hoped. They were clearly eager to be done with this activity. Finally, my oldest said, "Can we just do this later?" I sighed, and they bolted out of the kitchen and ran to the trampoline.

I was left at the kitchen table, alone and distraught. *Was there nothing they were excited to learn?*

WHERE HAS ALL THE CURIOSITY GONE?

I thought back to when the boys were young. They explored and played all day learning about whatever topics captured their imaginations. Maybe it was trains, cars, dinosaurs, or horses. It was easy to follow their natural curiosities, and we did what many parents and caregivers do: we nurtured their curiosity.

But something dramatic happened when my boys began attending school—maybe it happened in your family, too. The paradigm of learning changed. Natural inquiry was sidelined for standardization. They were no longer free to follow their natural curiosities to guide learning. Instead, from the moment they entered school, they had to learn what they were told. Learning transitioned from intrinsically to extrinsically motivated. Suddenly correct answers mattered, test scores quantified learning, and grades were set in stone.

My children, who had spent the first years of their lives learning with delight, were suddenly forced to learn a standardized curriculum at the expense of their own curiosities. I worried that over time, this had a damaging impact. Did it cause them to lose interest in learning? Did it silence their natural curiosities? Had they completely forgotten what it feels like to be driven by a sense of wonder? Did they no longer feel the insatiable need to know why? Had they stopped responding to the stirrings of their own hearts? Did school kill their curiosity?

In the future would they be lost, like so many adults who walk through life disconnected from passion and purpose? Would they buy best-selling books like *The Passion Test*, listen to podcasts, commiserate with coworkers, and visit life coaches and psychologists, on a mission to find meaning? Would these experts encourage them to reflect on their own childhoods to reconnect with their natural curiosities and passions to explore why, when, and how they disappeared? Did I still have time to rekindle the sparks of curiosity that had shone brightly before they were dimmed by school?

I worked myself up into a frenzy. This was no longer just a homeschooling sabbatical; it was a rescue mission to resuscitate curiosity!

Meanwhile, my carefree children happily played outside, enjoying the Wonder of free time. Through the window, I watched as they attempted flips on the trampoline, dug in the mulch, went backward down the slide while throwing a football in the air, and daydreamed on the swings. I invented a story that school had crushed their curiosity, but there it was right before my eyes.

CURIOSITY CANNOT BE FORCED

Curiosity is the engine that drives learning—from the inside out. Curiosity relies on intrinsic desire for knowledge and understanding. If curiosity is a blooming garden, then motivation is the water and sunlight that help it grow. I mistakenly believed that my children's curiosity could be forced, that motivation to learn would magically show up. This is not true. Curiosity cannot be forced—but it can be grown from within.

> Curiosity cannot be forced—but it can be grown from within.

Had I known then what I know now, I would not have asked for a top-ten list of curiosities on the spot at the kitchen table. Teresa Amabile, Constance Noonan Hadley, and Steven J. Kramer, researchers at Harvard Business School, showed that people under pressure are less able to be creative because they worry about how they will perform.[24] Sitting my children down and asking that they create a list of curiosities on the spot was the worst thing I could have done. Imagine the pressure I created in their young minds.

CURIOSITY STARTS AS A FLICKER, NOT A FLAME

When my children went outside to play, they serendipitously got the gift of free time, and with it a flicker of curiosity appeared. The boys came inside for a water break and asked, "Can we learn stuff that we never learned in school?"

"Yes!" I exclaimed.

Then they asked, "How do we find out about other things to learn?"

I suddenly remembered a picture my meditation teacher showed me in college. It was a pie chart that represented all possible knowledge. When she showed it to me, I felt the world open in a new way. I found it online, printed it out, and showed it to the boys.

THE PIE CHART OF POSSIBLE KNOWLEDGE

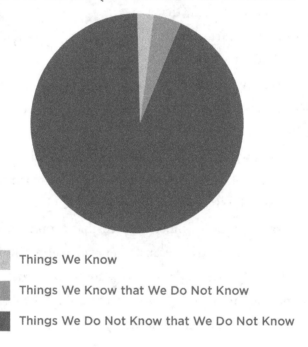

■ Things We Know

■ Things We Know that We Do Not Know

■ Things We Do Not Know that We Do Not Know

We talked about how the smallest wedge of the pie represents what we know. The boys reflected on the things they know, like fishing and reading and writing. Then we noticed that the next biggest wedge is the things we know we do not know. They named things like how to play lacrosse, how to play chess, what it is like in Antarctica, and how to do calculus. I explained that this piece of pie is a place to visit to ignite curiosity.

Then we talked about the biggest piece of the pie: the things we do not know that we do not know. They had a hard time with this category and asked me for an example. I shared something from a recent article I read about how scientists believe that the planets, stars, and everything you can see are less than 5 percent of the universe. "What is the other 95 percent?" they wondered. I told them that scientists think that invisible dark matter accounts for the other 95 percent of the universe's total energy and mass. They stared at me wide-eyed, and then my oldest asked, "What is dark matter?"

Yes! I wanted to flip on the trampoline! Curiosity was emerging. That simple question led to a trip to see *Dark Universe* at our local planetarium, a film about dark matter narrated by astrophysicist Neil deGrasse Tyson, which led to questions about astrophysics, which led to a late-night viewing of the stars in our own backyard.

CURIOSITY GROWS EXPONENTIALLY

Later that week, I introduced them to Buckminster Fuller's Knowledge Doubling Curve. Fuller, a twentieth-century inventor, noticed that until the year 1900, human knowledge doubled approximately every one hundred years. By the end of World War II, human knowledge was doubling every twenty-five years. Today, human knowledge doubles every twelve months. According to IBM, the build-out of the "internet of things" will lead to the doubling of knowledge every twelve hours.[25]

THE KNOWLEDGE DOUBLING CURVE

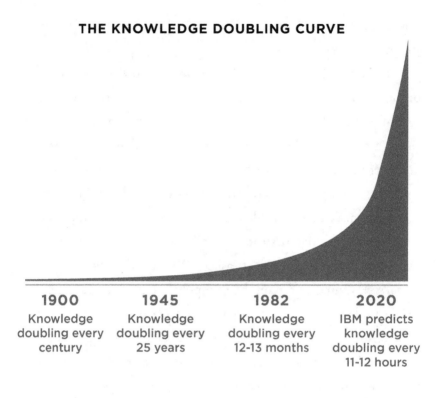

1900	1945	1982	2020
Knowledge doubling every century	Knowledge doubling every 25 years	Knowledge doubling every 12-13 months	IBM predicts knowledge doubling every 11-12 hours

The boys understood that if knowledge doubles every year, then it will be twice as large each year they move up in school.

I asked them, "How might that impact you as students?"

They asked me, "If knowledge grows so fast, how can people learn fast enough? How can teachers even decide what to teach?" I loved their mind-expanding questions.

They asked me, "Are there things to learn now that were not available when you were in school?" So I showed them an online course catalog from my alma mater, Northwestern University.

First, they were shocked that it was 277 pages. As they clicked through, they called out course titles in disbelief. "Plant Evolution and Diversity!" "Yiddish Culture!" "Introduction to Topology!" "Opera Singing!" and "The Science of Emotional Intelligence!" When they started to comprehend how vast knowledge is, the shackles came off.

"Why can't we learn stuff like this in school?" they asked.

"You can!" I exclaimed.

We browsed hundreds of unique subjects offered by The Great Courses, both online and on television.[26] We watched documentaries, went to the bookstore, and looked at classes at our community center and local art school. We perused classes online at K12.com and Johns Hopkins Center for Talented Youth. We watched *BrainPop*, *Popular Science for Kids*, *National Geographic*, *The Magic School Bus,* and even *Dude Perfect*.

CURIOSITY EMERGES

Surprisingly, a few weeks later, their lists of curiosities came unprompted. They were not written in a tidy list in their "curiosity journals" but scrawled on scrap paper found in the moment. The lists included curiosities about fishing in different ecosystems, website design and programming, optical illusions and magic tricks, drawing and painting, ocean life and the water cycle, mountain biking, how remote controls work, and outdoor activities, to name just a few. These raw and natural curiosities formed the backdrop to our home-schooling year.

THE WORLD IS YOUR CLASSROOM

My children's messy curiosity lists led to some of the greatest moments in our homeschooling year. For one, we embarked on a yearlong fishing journey that took us to dozens of ponds and streams in Maryland, as well as rivers and lakes across the United States. At each, we charted water pH using a simple swimming pool kit, time of day, wind speed, type of bait, water conditions, and what we caught. This led to exploring YouTube, which led to a passion for video editing and motion graphics, which has opened many unexpected doors for my oldest son.

My middle son's list led to a fascination with making and testing vehicles and gadgets in what came to be known as "the experiment laboratory." (It was actually a folding table in the garage.) Here, he invented magic tricks, developed CO_2 cars and rocket launchers, built a working replica of Michael Jackson's antigravity lean with custom tricked-out boots, and performed a myriad of other science experiments. He also started experimenting with music, which is now a big part of his life.

The love of nature that showed up on both lists led to a yearlong exploration of national parks where we held banana slugs, stood on volcanoes, climbed into caves to see Native American art, and learned how the Joshua Tree inspired Dr. Seuss's *The Lorax*.

CURIOSITY DEFIES SUBJECT AREAS

Did these adventures fall neatly into the subject areas of science, humanities, physical education, and art? No. Instead, they captured the beautifully diverse intersections of true learning. In the real world, everything is interconnected. Dividing math, science, literature, art, language, and history into separate subject areas is completely artificial. Yet in school, we "learn" in thirty to sixty-minute increments, with strict boundaries between subjects, rarely connecting them to one another. Think about it: How often does your child talk about the intersection of Shakespeare and math, physics and basketball, American history and music? Outside the school building, our kids are more apt to discover and explore some of these new connections.

Here's an example of how curiosity led to an unexpected connection for my youngest son.

Through the years, we've taken many walks down our driveway of doom—so called because every spring hundreds of spiky green balls fall from the tree branches and scatter on the ground. They gradually dry out and become spiky foot bombs. During quarantine, the dog hurt his paw on one, I twisted my ankle on one, and my youngest son flew off his bike when his front tires hit a cluster.

One day, we gathered several in our T-shirts and brought them back to the kitchen. We looked up "spiky seed balls." Turns out, they are the seed pods from the sweet gum tree. The scary-looking outer shell has dozens of hard, prickly points that eventually open to let the seeds out. As one gardening blogger described them, these "hard, brown, spiky balls create some serious hazards. Not only can they wound you if you slip and fall into them, they can also roll unexpectedly, causing sprained ankles." Their spikes make them hard to rake up, and the blogger warned against riding over them with a lawnmower, as "when airborne they are as dangerous as grenades."[27] Digging deeper, we also learned that the inside of the seeds contain shikimic acid, the secret ingredient in the flu-fighting drug Tamiflu.[28]

We wondered: what can we do with these spiky balls? My youngest, who had just watched *Home Alone*, jokingly suggested that we use them to make a booby trap. With that little burst of curiosity satisfied, he went about his business. The seed pods stayed on the kitchen counter for several days. Occasionally, I saw him sticking them together like Velcro.

Several weeks later, my youngest son ran into my bedroom. He had seen the image of coronavirus created by the CDC, the gray ball dotted with red spikes, which has become an unofficial logo of the pandemic. He noticed that the external structure on the virus had crownlike spikes. "The pods of doom are like coronavirus!" he said. His curious observation was spot on. Researchers across the world were looking at the spike proteins on the surface of the virus to understand how they attach, fuse, and gain entry to cells. Curiosity, innate in all our children, is vital in developing new approaches to solve real-world problems and just might lead to breakthrough ideas.

> **Curiosity, innate in all our children, is vital in developing new approaches to solve real-world problems.**

FANNING THE SPARK

Curiosity makes our children feel alive and engaged. It helps them make connections, Kashdan notes, and allows them to experience moments of insight and meaning—all of which provide the foundation for joyful learning.[29] As parents, what can we do to help foster curiosity during the pandemic and beyond? Here are five ways that you can fan the spark.

1. **Watch for a flicker of curiosity**. As your children settle into free time, watch carefully for fleeting moments when curiosity starts to show up. What questions do your children ask? What do they talk about with their friends? What do they complain about? What do they get excited about? Lean into whatever shows up, even if it is not something *you* are excited about. For example, say your child seems only to be interested in video games. At dinner, engage them in conversation about their favorite video game. What do they like about it? Do they want to learn how to program or design or write video games? Somewhere in there may be the spark of curiosity.

2. **Listen to and elicit questions, but don't jump in with answers.** As parents, we can be too quick to provide advice, opinions, and answers. To foster curiosity, try to hold back, ask questions, and listen. In an article for the *Harvard Educational Review*, Susan Engel of Williams College argues for the promotion of curiosity in schools, calling for a "shift in the way we see the traditional role of a teacher, from one who answers questions to one who elicits them."[30] Let this be your guiding principle; eliciting questions will uncover a treasure trove of curiosity.

> You can find a list of seventy-five open-ended questions in Appendix III.

3. **Encourage your child to spend time on their questions.** When your child asks a question with a nonobvious answer—something many of us have experienced during the pandemic—encourage them to stick with it. It's OK to admit that the answer is unknown while also praising them for asking a relevant and thoughtful question. Show approval when your children are willing to spend time on an open-ended question, grapple with it, share it with others, and build on it. These questions are not a waste of time and can ultimately lead to something rewarding and worthwhile.

4. **Stay with your child's curiosities and questions, even if the subject matter does not interest you.** Perhaps your child will become interested in something unexpected, something you wouldn't necessarily have chosen for them. Let them follow their curiosity. Who knows where it might lead? As the late Steve Jobs said, "Much of what I stumbled into by following my curiosity and intuition turned out to be priceless later on." Don't limit

any of the million pathways your child might follow to find what stirs their heart. You already have that intuition to nurture your child's interests and passions, which in turn nurture their curiosity. Just follow where their excitement leads—whether it be trucks or dinosaurs, rainbows or unicorns, cooking or pottery.

5. **Above all, don't be annoyed when your child asks questions.** We all know the exhaustion of responding to a million questions. Change your perspective from seeing this behavior as a nuisance to seeing this behavior as a blessing. Notice when your child asks the same question over and over, and help them find out how to seek and pursue different answers. Or try answering their questions with more questions. Notice and praise the weird and offbeat questions too. The seemingly silly or strange questions often result in the biggest breakthroughs. Always have some thought-provoking questions in your back pocket. A well-placed question by a parent can change any aspect of life in a moment and just might unlock something wondrous for your child.

> A well-placed question by a parent can change any aspect of life in a moment and just might unlock something wondrous for your child.

CURIOSITY IS CONTAGIOUS

Remember, simply asking questions inspires others to ask questions. The contagiousness of curiosity was demonstrated by a team at the Massachusetts Institute of Technology who found that "a robot that expressed enthusiasm for learning and actively ask[ed] questions about a story's outcome during a reading activity with a child inspire[d] that child's desire for knowledge."[31]

Sometimes all it takes to reignite that pilot light is a ping-pong match of questions. One question reveals a hundred more. New passions become launchpads for more questions. And as questions become deeper and deeper, they might ultimately lead to ideas that will change the world, like a cure for a disease or a technology that will ensure the survival of our species.

Curiosity is also what builds the bridge to our next Wonder: making. As Aristotle said, "For the things we have to learn before we can do them, we learn by doing them."

KEY TAKEAWAYS

- Curiosity is born from free time and leads to questions.

- Curiosity is a natural, innate spark that requires no special training.

- Expressing curiosity lights up the reward and pleasure circuit in our brains and is scientifically linked with fulfillment and joy.

- Being told the right answers stifles the natural emergence of curiosity.

- Curiosity cannot be forced, but it can be nurtured. It is tied to intrinsic motivation.

- Curiosity, like knowledge, is exponential.

- Curiosity is sparked by the intersection and collision of subject areas.

- Parents should not rely on the school system to ignite curiosity in children.

- Curiosity is contagious.

WHAT NEXT? FIVE WAYS TO BRING THIS CHAPTER TO LIFE

- **Think:** Prepandemic, what was your child most curious about in school? During quarantine, did any new curiosities emerge? Name five things that you have seen your child get excited and curious about in recent months. What can you do to deepen curiosity in these areas?

- **Feel:** How did you feel the last time you were deeply curious about something? How did it feel to pursue or not pursue that curiosity? Talk to your child about how they might develop and follow their own curiosity. What emotions show up for them, and for you?

- **Do:** Give your child a no-pressure curiosity journal. Encourage them to jot down any questions they have—about anything and everything—thoughts they want to follow, or perhaps things they want to look into or know more about. It doesn't matter how big or how small the topic is, or whether it's part of a school curriculum or something they saw on YouTube or on TikTok. Alternatively, start a curiosity jar for the entire family. Anytime someone has a question, ask them to write it on a piece of paper and drop it in the jar.

- **Act:** Play the question game with your child. Pick an object, any object, and try to come up with twenty-five questions about it in five minutes. No repeats or yes-or-no questions allowed! Don't be surprised if this is hard at first; children are not usually expected to flex their question-asking muscles. If your child needs some encouragement, remind them about the five Ws: who, what, when, where, and why, plus how. *Why* and *how* often lead to the most curious questions.

- **Discuss:** Ask your child what they are curious about. Just listen and ask questions. Don't judge or offer advice; just follow them, wherever it leads.

PERSONAL CHECK-IN:
WHAT ARE YOU THINKING?

- What was my child the most curious about when they were very young? What is my child the most curious about today? How can I better understand what my child is curious about?

- What simple steps can I take every day to ignite my child's curiosity?

- What curiosity-building questions from Appendix III can I ask my child to deepen their curiosity?

MAKING

Tell me, and I will not forget; show me, and I may remember; but involve me, and I will understand.

—CHINESE PROVERB

In the first months of the pandemic, many of us—adults and children alike—turned to the digital world for comfort, for company, and entertainment. As we left behind our hectic schedules and embraced free time and curiosity, something strange and wonderful also happened: we started making things.

People who had never picked up a needle and thread started making masks. People who rarely used their ovens started baking banana bread and experimenting with sourdough starters. When toilet paper and hand sanitizer sold out, so did flour and yeast!

Alongside baking pans, children started picking up paintbrushes, colored pencils, and clay. With a surge in making art, the rate of new enrollments in Virtual Art Academy jumped to five times more enrollment than the previous twelve months—the most dramatic increase ever seen in the thirteen years the academy has been running.[32] Social media became an artistic outlet, with people showing off time-lapse works of art on TikTok and Instagram. The hashtag #quarantineart emerged and saw an overwhelming number of posts. With fewer distractions and increased downtime, children picked up instruments, started gardens, took up woodworking, experimented with photography and stop-motion animation, and learned all kind of dances. Writers everywhere took on book projects—including me.

This explosion in making is verifiable. Between the middle of March and the middle of April 2020, Google searches for "How to make" doubled, as did searches for "DIY."[33] It was almost as if, as our lives moved entirely online, we felt the primal urge to do what humans have always done: *make* things. Real things. Tangible things. In a world that abruptly became even more virtual than we were accustomed to, we all wanted to be *hands-on*.

> **Between the middle of March and the middle of April 2020, Google searches for "How to make" doubled, as did searches for "DIY."**

WHAT DO YOUR CHILD'S HANDS DO?

That's what *making* really means: having hands-on experiences. It could be taking apart a computer or a vacuum cleaner and putting it back together. It could be building a makeshift home gym. It could be drawing pictures. It could be baking a pie. It could be collecting rocks on a walk through the neighborhood. It could be studying the different kinds of bugs in the backyard or making a fort. Whatever it is, wherever curiosity leads, it is something done with your hands.

For much of history, human beings have spent most of their days *doing*—using their hands and making things. Only for the last hundred years or so, as human culture shifted from agriculture to industry to the information age, have people spent more of the day sitting down. And it has only been in the last thirty years or so that human culture has shifted to people spending most of their days staring at screens.

During the pandemic I contributed to a worldwide broadcast event called *The Call to Unite*, which featured Oprah Winfrey, Jennifer Garner, Deepak Chopra, Yo-Yo Ma, and many others. There were several wonderful guests, but singer-songwriter Jewel touched my heart. She shared a story about how she pulled herself out of homelessness and hardship. It started, she revealed, with watching her own hands: "Your hands are the servants of your thoughts," she said in the broadcast, "so if you want to see what you're thinking, watch what your hands are doing, because it's your thoughts cooled down into action."[34]

Prepandemic, what would it look like if you followed your child's hands through their day at school and home? What about now, during the pandemic? How much of their time do they spend using their hands for anything other than homework or on-screen activities? How much of their schooling and education is spent doing anything hands-on and actually *making*?

OUR HOMESCHOOL YEAR: HANDS-ON VERSUS HEADS-DOWN

When our homeschool year began, I was surprised to learn that my children associated learning not with being hands-on, but with being "heads-down." While their elementary school promised experiential programs, my children had few opportunities for true hands-on learning. They spent most of the school day seated in chairs, working at a table or a desk, and reading workbooks or doing worksheets. Sometimes, the worksheets were replaced with iPads or laptops, but the experience was still "heads-down."

Unsurprisingly, my children didn't want to spend the homeschool year sitting down and looking down. Once we ignited their curiosity, they wanted to go places, make stuff, and get outside. They wanted to *do* something. So we decided to make experiential learning a priority and strived to be more hands-on in a heads-down world.

> **We decided to make experiential learning a priority and strived to be more hands-on in a heads-down world.**

To us, being hands-on meant *doing things* rather than learning only from books, videos, or the internet. In contrast, being heads-down meant sitting and looking down, whether it was at a workbook, an iPhone, or a computer screen. While we knew we could not eliminate all table-based learning, we wanted to minimize it. So we set a goal of sitting at a table or desk for no more than two hours per day, allowing us to be active the rest of the day.

We broke our hands-on learning into two categories: experiments and field trips. Later in this chapter, in the field trip section, I will also share ideas for virtual field trips available to children during the pandemic.

EXPERIMENTS: BUILDING THE "BACK ROOM"

When it came to experiments, my husband was delighted to share his love of hands-on learning with the boys. You see, my husband is a kind of inventor, although he would not describe himself in that way. He fidgets, tinkers, disassembles, alters, experiments, reassembles, and endlessly tweaks, adjusts, and fixes anything and everything. He has a way of looking at something and taking it apart in his head until he finds a way to make it better.

One day, as we reflected on the difference between homeschool and traditional school, my husband shared a fond recollection of what he called his "back room," a small, dusty, forgotten space that was half attic, half closet. It was a space most adults would use to store holiday decorations. But in his eyes, it was an amazing, private hideaway where there was no oversight, no rules, and no mistakes.

In this magical space, he took apart old electronics and rewired them to do wacky things. His mom allowed him to use the space as an audio/visual laboratory. She only entered to stock a small refrigerator with snacks and soda. It was a haven for his imagination, and the place where ideas were born. He remembers countless hours spent in his "back room" experimenting with old parts to see what kind of things he could create. He once rigged a light switch to answer the telephone, turn on music, and open the refrigerator. He hacked into a touch-tone phone and used the keypad to control various machines. This back room was a place of hands-on learning, where he taught himself how to rig home automation systems and become a musician; he even started a lucrative DJ business.

Truth be told, he also lit the forest next to his house on fire, created several small explosions, shocked himself silly with a nine-volt battery, and made plenty of messy mistakes. I'm sure there were days when his mother was ready to lock up his back room, but she didn't. She gave him space and a place for his dreams to hatch. The back room was a place where he could explore his passions, take risks, fail, and make a mess with no one looking over his shoulder—even as he used power tools all by himself. It was a place of hands-on exploration and discovery, where curiosity reigned and where he was able to create the ideas from his own mind.

These passions manifested later in life when he went to the University of Miami to study music and audio engineering, and later toured the globe with musical artists. Now, as cofounder of our creative agency, he applies his technical ingenuity and hands-on expertise to create large-scale live and digital experiences for the world's biggest brands.

He lamented that children today do not have back rooms to get hands-on with their passions. He felt strongly that every child should have their own place to explore and create, whether it is a small closet, a corner of the garage, or a nook behind the sofa. So, he made it a priority to create some version of a "back room" for each of our children.

My oldest son wanted his back room to be an editing and motion graphics desk where he could make videos. This became the launchpad for his current passion of making sports videos.

My middle son started with "the experiment laboratory," a folding table in the garage. We stocked it with used electronic parts, craft and art supplies, old water bottles, recycled junk, and duct tape. Here, he built gadgets, model rockets, and even played around with the once-viral "hot knife challenge." Then, as his music passion grew, he moved the folding table into his bedroom to write and record music.

It was not long before the boys started combining the resources of their two back rooms. My middle son performed strange experiments like melting flip-flops and launching raw eggs with clever contraptions, while my oldest captured the process on video and then edited the clips together. Having these hands-on spaces fostered their own methods of self-expression and creativity.

They became obsessed with hands-on learning. Even when we visited Grandpa and Nona in Florida, they were ready for more hands-on challenges. Grandpa taught them about OODA loops, a problem-solving model developed by a former US Air Force officer, and George Pólya's four-step problem-solving method. He challenged the boys to solve hands-on problems with these methods. The first challenge, called Fly the Plane, dared them to see if a broken remote could be fixed to fly a remote-control plane. The next challenge provoked them to repair a broken air filter. Nona also taught them hands-on food science, including how to extract iron from cereal with a magnet.

These back rooms gave them a place to experiment and "think with their hands." They were so successful that when our children returned to school, we kept their back rooms going—and they are still going to this day! Even my youngest son now has a back room: a tiny storage closet under the stairs where he reclines on a dog bed under LED string lights to hatch plans, hide his treasure, and set his imagination free. As he grows, it will be fun to follow his curiosities and see how his back room changes over time.

> Want ideas for how to make an easy
> "back room" for your child? See Appendix IV.

FIELD TRIPS: LET'S GO OUTSIDE!

The other category of hands-on learning is field trips. We visited parks, museums, bakeries, and bookstores. We defined any outing as learning, so even a trip to Home Depot or the garden center was special. This variety of experiences created an amazing fabric of learning.

But our most exciting field trips were visits to the national parks. With work related travel taking us out west, we were fortunate to have the means to use our homeschooling year to explore several national parks—including the Black Canyon of the Gunnison, Redwood National Park, Rogue River Valley, Yellowstone, and many others in between.

These visits brought to life the breathtaking and diverse geography of our country, and the rich and humbling diversity of our people. The geological story of America came to life like no history book could capture, unfolding before our eyes and under our feet. The children learned how the collision of tectonic plates created mountain ranges. They saw how the erosive power of water carved giant canyons, and how oceans dried to become barren rock formations. In driving across the country, they saw population density and population scarcity. They saw wind turbines, solar fields, and nuclear power plants. They learned about botany, zoology, atmospheric science, wildlife preservation, and weather patterns. They began to contemplate the role that humans have played in these landscapes throughout time and to consider the influence humans will have in the future.

These national park experiences also led to new curiosities. For example, my oldest son was inspired to complete the Maryland Hunter Safety Course to earn a hunting license. While our family does not hunt, he wanted to learn about wildlife conservation and understand the role he could play as a steward of our natural resources. Both older boys, avid fishermen, were inspired to take a Coast Guard–approved boaters' safety course and earn boating licenses. Also, with so much time spent in nature, they asked to become certified in CPR and first aid to learn the critical skills needed to respond to an emergency.

VIRTUAL FIELD TRIPS DURING THE PANDEMIC

Today, COVID-19 travel, social distancing, and capacity restrictions mean that physical field trips are not always possible. However, there are more options than ever before for virtual field trips. Here's a list of ten ideas to get you started, including many that are free.

1. **Virtual Visit to the National Parks.** The National Park Service offers several virtual field trips, tours, and videos on their website, including options for live guided tours and live video feeds, such as real-time wildlife cams. For younger kids, the National Park Service Junior Ranger program offers even more options to explore national parks online and provides activities that kids can complete at home.

2. **Virtual Historical Tours.** If you've ever wanted to take your child to a historical site, you're in luck, because many have created virtual tours to encourage "visitors" during the pandemic. Consider a virtual historical tour at The White House, Mount Vernon, Colonial Williamsburg, Ellis Island, the Vatican, Buckingham Palace, Stonehenge, or Machu Pichu. Perform a Google search for "virtual tour" plus your desired destination and then sign up for the tour. You might end up at the Great Wall of China, the Great Pyramids of Giza, the Taj Mahal, or Niagara Falls.

3. **Virtual Museum Experiences.** Many famous museums, like the Louvre and Smithsonian, offer free virtual visits. Some local and regional museums are following suit. Check your local art, history, and children's museums for virtual offerings. Then expand to museums all over the world, including the British Museum in London, the National Museum of Modern and Contemporary Art in Seoul, the Van Gogh Museum in Amsterdam, the Guggenheim Museum in New York, or the Pergamon Museum in Berlin. Remember that many museums offer free downloadable activities like coloring pages, puzzles and writing prompts.

4. **Science Centers.** Many science centers have taken their programs online to help kids get hands-on at home. For example, NASA

offers many STEM activities for grades K to 4, ranging from building foam rockets to solving space station emoji puzzles. Take a virtual visit to NASA's Langley Research Center, the Museum of Science in Boston, the Saint Louis Science Center, Belgium's Museum of Natural Sciences, Oxford University's History of Science Museum, the National Museum of Computing, or the Museo Galileo in Florence, Italy.

5. **Discovery Education.** The website of Discovery Education offers free virtual field trips with companion guides and hands-on learning activities. For example, kids can go behind the scenes at the Johnson Space Center in Houston, Texas, or visit the National Basketball Association headquarters or experience the Canadian tundra for the annual polar bear migration. After watching pre-recorded videos, students complete activities associated with the virtual trip.

6. **Virtual Visits to Zoos and Aquariums.** Even if your local zoo is closed, your child can still get up close with animals. Zoos around the world offer live cams, virtual behind-the-scenes tours, and activities for kids. For example, watch the giant panda cam at the National Zoo in Washington, DC. Or visit the Bronx Zoo for virtual encounters with sloths, cheetahs, and camels. The San Diego Zoo has many live cams to choose from, including the exhibits of penguins, tigers, koalas, and giraffes. The Monterey Bay Aquarium offers live cams of everything from sharks to birds in the aviary. Shedd Aquarium offers virtual meet-and-greets with sea lions, penguins, and otters.

7. **Virtual Story Time.** Virtual story time has taken off during the pandemic. Many public libraries, including New York Public Library, offer virtual story times to bring the joy of reading

to kids at home. Librarians read books, sing songs, and keep kids engaged with reading. On Twitter, entertainer Josh Gad offers ten-minute story times as he reads classics like *The Day the Crayons Quit* by Drew Daywalt and *The Giving Tree* by Shel Silverstein. On the *Read Together, Be Together* website, celebrities like Jennifer Garner and Alan Cumming read stories to kids. Of course, YouTube also offers many wonderful read-aloud stories.

8. **Virtual Farm and Dairy Visits.** Some farms and dairies also now offer virtual tours for families. Your child can experience life on a Vermont dairy farm through the *Billings Farm at Home* website. Also check out online video tours of Talview Farm, Dutch Hollow Farm, and Will-O-Crest Farm. Do a Google search for "virtual farm tour" in your own state for additional offerings.

9. **Airbnb.** Airbnb may be known as a vacation rental company, but it also offers hundreds of virtual fieldtrips. Your child can take a class with a member of the US Olympic team, learn about animals from experts, or uncover ruins with an archaeologist. Most experiences have a per-person charge, but some are free.

10. **Amazon Explore.** In late September 2020, Amazon launched a new service called Amazon Explore that allows people to book live, virtual experiences led by local experts. For example, your child can check out toucans and sloths at a Costa Rican animal rescue, learn how to make sushi, or explore the Freedom Trail in Boston. Amazon Explore is a one-on-one experience in which your child interacts with a guide. Prices vary, and most sessions last about an hour.

THE IMPORTANCE OF OUTSIDE TIME

Another type of field trip is the one in your own backyard. Nature is an amazing way to get hands-on, and it is accessible and free to everyone. Simply being out in nature is a hugely beneficial aspect of experiential learning.

Growing up in Colorado, I was always drawn to open spaces and outdoor recreation. As part of the generation that played outside, I yearned for my children to enjoy the simple pleasures of an outdoor life: hiking, biking, fishing, camping, and just playing outside in the neighborhood.

In my childhood, our street was alive with the sounds of kids playing until well after dark. But before the pandemic, our family rarely heard children playing outside. Many of today's parents can relate to quiet neighborhood streets as childhood has shifted largely indoors.

A recent study by the Nature Conservancy is disheartening, as it reveals that before the pandemic, only 10 percent of children spent time outdoors each day.[35] Their precious hours were consumed by school, activities, indoor play, and screen time. To put it in perspective, each day, the average American child was said to spend less than twenty minutes of unstructured free play outdoors, and up to seven hours in front of a screen.[36]

> **The average American child was said to spend less than twenty minutes of unstructured free play outdoors.**

Prepandemic, children spent less time outdoors than literal prisoners. In the United States, inmates in maximum-security prison are guaranteed two hours of outdoor time per day. Meanwhile, a survey of twelve thousand parents in ten countries found that 50 percent of children aged five to twelve spend less than an hour outside daily, and one-third spend thirty minutes or less outside each day.[37] This sounds shocking, but it's not surprising based on the hectic schedules we talked about in chapter 2. What is normally offered in a regular school day—a fifteen-minute recess break or a forty-minute PE class—is completely inadequate. Parents, this also applies to us. According to the Harvard School of Public Health, American adults spend more time inside vehicles than they do outdoors.[38]

Some health professionals refer to this lack of outdoor time as "nature deficit disorder." Research shows that a lack of time outdoors contributes to childhood obesity, diabetes, vitamin deficiencies, asthma, and even vision problems.[39] The good news is that these negative effects are easy to address by simply getting outside. A 2018 report by the University of East Anglia that analyzed global data involving more than 290 million people found that "spending time in, or living close to, natural green spaces is associated with diverse and significant health benefits. It reduces the risk of type II diabetes, cardiovascular disease, premature death, and increases sleep duration."[40] The health benefits of being outside are so great that some pediatricians even prescribe outside time as part of the healing and recovery process for children.[41]

Nature is not only beneficial for children's physical health, but also their mental health. Many studies have shown that nature reduces psychological stress levels.[42] The University of East Anglia report found that "people living closer to nature also had reduced diastolic blood pressure, heart rate and stress. In fact, one of the really interesting things we found is that exposure to greenspace significantly reduces people's levels of salivary cortisol—a physiological marker of stress."[43]

As a parent, I know that my own children are happier and more relaxed when they play outside. When they get closer to nature, whether it be the old oak tree in the backyard, a neighborhood fishing pond, or a walking trail, they just unwind.

Nature also sparks the curiosity we talked about in chapter 3. The things children observe in the natural world are diverse and interesting and a source of infinite questions. And because there is less structure in outdoor play, children naturally become more curious and creative. After three days of backpacking in the wilderness, Outward Bound participants performed 50 percent better on creative problem-solving tasks.[44] Nature is the perfect way to participate in hands-on experiential learning because nature activates more sensory stimulation than being indoors. There is simply more to see, hear, smell, touch, and do—which is the Wonder of this chapter!

> **Because there is less structure in outdoor play, children naturally become more curious and creative.**

REDISCOVERING THE OUTDOORS IN THE PANDEMIC

Surprisingly, the pandemic prompted us to get outside in ways we hadn't before. In the early days of shelter-in-place restrictions, going for a walk outside or a hike in the woods felt safe. Even in densely populated urban areas, people stepped out into the fresh air with proper social distancing. *Outside* was one of the few places left for our children to go.

All of a sudden, entire families went for long, leisurely walks. For many, the joy of being outside provided a crucial outlet to deal with fear and anxiety. Turning to nature to soothe raw emotions, people began connecting with neighbors, family members, pets, and the very ground we walk on. As a result of the pandemic, we rediscovered the healing power of nature.

With renewed interest in spending time outside, children eagerly began riding bikes again and we experienced an unexpected nation-wide bike shortage. At first, children in our neighborhood stayed close to home. Then, with masks on, they began to ride with neighborhood children on opposite sides of the street. Soon, many neighborhood streets and alleys were alive with bikes, skateboards, and scooters. Some parents loosened up rules and let their kids roam around the neighborhood in "biker squads" of all ages, reminiscent of the joys of our retro childhoods.

The good news is that as states began to lift restrictions, the walking and biking haven't stopped. It doesn't matter if you live in Manhattan or the Rocky Mountains; the pandemic has taught us that outdoor learning can happen right in your own backyard, no matter how big or small, or the park down the street—just like hands-on learning can happen in your basement, garage, or kitchen table. You can take a walk in the park—or down your street—and learn about the different trees and plants you see, just like my son and I did with the sweet gum tree we talked about in chapter 3. You can give your child a magnifying glass so they can closely examine the bugs in the backyard, identify them, and learn how they fit into the ecosystem. You can look up historical locations within walking or driving distance of your apartment or townhome, or take a mini–field trip through different city blocks to simply appreciate the sights and the sounds of the outdoor world.

HANDS-ON WITH TECHNOLOGY: CREATORS, NOT CONSUMERS

We've discussed how hands-on learning can happen outside and through physical making in a basement or a garage—but paradoxically, it can also happen using technology. Yes, I'm talking about using dreaded *screen time* in a productive, hands-on way. How can you do that? By encouraging your children to use their screens to be *creators*, not *consumers*.

As discussed in chapter 2, we live in a culture that encourages children to be consumers, not creators. They consume, consume, consume. They gobble up information, content, videos, social feeds, entertainment, and everything else we serve them. But did you know that for every one hundred people who are online—children in particular—ninety-nine are consuming, and only one is creating?[45] This is called the 1 percent rule. In other words, the vast majority of screen time for youth is spent consuming other people's content.

> **For every one hundred people who are online—children in particular—ninety-nine are consuming, and only one is creating.**

What is the difference between consuming and creating? It's as simple as it sounds: creators *create*, while consumers *consume* what is already created. For example, consumers watch YouTube; creators make the videos. Consumers listen to music; creators write and perform the music. Consumers play video games; creators design and make the games.

One by-product of the accelerated adoption of technology during the pandemic is all the new technological skills children are learning that can help them be creators. For example, a friend told me that her once camera-shy daughter now looks forward to participating in virtual classes with custom green screen backgrounds. She also loves to use the whiteboard features to draw and annotate on shared documents with her friends. Even my eight-year-old can start a Zoom meeting and facilitate a screen share with multiple presenters while "air playing" to the television. From the perspective of hands-on learning, we should encourage our children to learn about new technologies with the expectation that they will create, not just consume. For example, they can make their own apps or games, experiment with virtual reality, create their own movies and videos, or write and post music. Some social media platforms provide exciting opportunities for children to create in collaboration with other creators. For example, my middle son enjoys making cooking video duets on TikTok.

THE INTERNET AS A RESOURCE FOR MAKING

Even if your child is not interested in learning new technologies, programming, or coding and designing apps, technology can still be used to inspire hands-on learning.

During the pandemic, virtual learning resources have exploded. According to reports by KPMG and Google, the educational technology sector is growing exponentially, projected to reach an estimated $2 billion in 2021.[46] The proliferation of online resources has connected us with, quite literally, the whole world. For example, when homeschooling my youngest son, we use BrainPop.com, K12.com, and IXL.com to learn online. One of our favorite resources is Outschool.com, a platform that offers very low-cost virtual classes on every subject imaginable. For example, my youngest son took a virtual field trip to Easter Island. He journeyed through virtual math escape rooms, conducted science experiments, and made elaborate art projects. He even joined an expert-led online class about training service dogs and put this knowledge into practice with our own dog.

My middle son started taking voice lessons online from a woman in California. That same son participated in the world finals of Odyssey of the Mind. His team had to adapt their final theatrical performance into a digital format using Zoom—a perfect example of the creative collaboration that can happen online when in-person collaboration isn't possible.

The internet opens the door to infinite possibilities of learning. While there are proven dangers in using screen time for consumption, we can be more encouraging of screen time for curiosity. The internet is undoubtedly a resource worth utilizing to explore questions. It offers the immediacy of having anyone and anything at your fingertips right from your own screen. It builds a bridge to expert teachers all over the world. You can learn African drumming from someone in Nigeria, Indian cooking from someone in Mumbai, Chinese from someone in Hong Kong, as easily as you take photography lessons from a teacher in New York City. Time zones are no longer a barrier for learning either as popular platforms like Udemy, Teachable, Thinkific, and Kajabi allow experts to create their courses on-demand.

The internet offers the opportunity for your children to interact and develop meaningful learning connections with people outside the classroom—even if it's just for a one-time lesson or short-term class. The ideas of microlearning and micromentorship are taking hold and will transform the future of learning. Prepandemic, it was less common for children to have bite-size interactions with people who can guide, inspire, and teach them. Today, whatever your child wants to learn, there is a teacher out there who can teach them. Today, my youngest son takes piano lessons on Zoom, my oldest meets with his hockey team's yoga instructor on Zoom, and I am taking dance classes on Zoom—all for less money than the very same in-person classes would cost. The access and immediacy are transformative and will certainly outlast the pandemic. And remember, there are heaps of free classes to take advantage of all over the web and on social media.

Of course, children can also do what so many adults have done during the pandemic: look up how-tos for just about anything. For example, my youngest son spent an hour watching tutorials on how to solve a Rubik's Cube. He's learned how to make Oobleck, a marshmallow tower, and a campfire. And like many kids his age, he also watches how-tos about all varieties of trick shots and bottle flips. Technology is an incredible conduit to help our children try new things.

EMBRACE THE MESS

The thought of your child looking up a recipe on YouTube and attempting to make it or creating a giant Rube Goldberg machine may make your heart leap into your mouth. *Won't they make a mess?*

The answer is yes. According to Joshua Block, a humanities teacher at Science Leadership Academy in Philadelphia, "Learning is a messy process—and authentic, project-based learning immerses us in unique parts of this mess."[47]

One thing is true about making: your children *will* make a mess. That's inevitable. If they're going to learn how to cook, they will make a mess in

> **One thing is true about making: your children *will* make a mess.**

the kitchen. If they're going to build an epic spider web with string and duct tape, or build an entire LEGO civilization, it might take over your whole house. The process of making, creating, and imagining is often messy.

When the pandemic hit, many of us found a lot more mess in our houses than we were used to. I'm not just talking about regular, everyday laundry and dishes; I'm talking about extended, multiday, big-project messes that show up and take over entire rooms for weeks at a time. As our children found ways to entertain themselves, we were forced to increase our tolerance for total-house-takeover messes of epic proportion. For example, about midway through the first month of quarantine, I came downstairs to find my living room taken over by an elaborate pillow fort interconnected by a web of duct tape and party streamers. Above it, shreds of toilet paper dangled from a spinning ceiling fan. (Of course, I saved the toilet paper.) This fort stayed for days until it was destroyed by a wrestling match.

A few weeks later, the art on one wall of my family room had been relocated to (by which I mean shoved against) another wall and replaced with a huge piece of green fabric duct-taped to the entire wall face. Here, my middle son had been experimenting with green screen backgrounds for Zoom. When I relayed these stories to a neighbor while walking the dog, she shared that her dining room, supposedly the fanciest room in her house, was now overrun with scribble-scrabbled cardboard boxes used as pretend appliances in an elaborate play kitchen for her younger daughter.

For many parents, these epic messes would not have met prepandemic household standards. For so many years, we outsourced the messy part of creativity to schools and extracurricular activities and messes in the home have become taboo. But the truth is, *making is messy.*

When my oldest son was young, he loved to draw and paint, and he burned through materials faster than I could replenish them. One day, I decided to stock up, so we headed to Target. I browsed the art aisle in search of crayons and markers when I saw something I had not seen before: row upon row of products from a line of children's art supplies called "No Mess." Each kit came with one special marker that was colorless. When the child colored on a special blank page, a picture would suddenly appear. The magic marker revealed a predrawn picture on the page.

I'm a marketer. I get it. This line of products fills a need. Parents don't want to clean up after the children. Voilà—enter no-mess art projects. But is this really what we want to teach our children?

Messes don't mean that our children are slobs. If we want to encourage making and hands-on learning, we need to embrace the mess that comes with it. When you feel the pain of stepping on LEGOs with bare feet; find flour dusted all over the kitchen counter, cabinets, and floor; or pull a bit of drywall off with the duct tape, try to see the bigger picture. Instead of immediately asking them to clean up, ask your kids about what they are trying to explore, experiment with, or discover. You might uncover that they are on a path of passion that will lead to wondrous new things.

After all, it was the willingness of Steven Spielberg's mother to let her son make a mess that launched him on his path to become one of the most successful filmmakers of all time. She allowed and encouraged him to make movies at home, no matter how messy they got. Once, she even helped him create convincing bloody ooze for a monster movie by cooking thirty cans of cherries in her pressure cooker until they exploded all over the kitchen![48]

Of course, we also need to live in our homes and keep our sanity—as well as maintain a safe and sanitary environment. Some mess can be mitigated by encouraging making to happen in a designated "back room," like we discussed earlier. But some creative messes may overflow into your main living area. Keep an open mind about where the mess is coming from, and what messes may be allowed to stick around for a little while to help your child learn.

EMBRACE MISTAKES AND FAILURE

While we've been talking about literal messes, there's another kind of messiness that comes with making: mistakes and failure. Being hands-on means trying something. And when you try something new, you might fail. You might do it wrong. In fact, if you're trying something for the first time, you are likely to make mistakes, or at least have room for improvement. Your children will too—and that is more than OK. It's part of the learning process. In fact, psychologist Jason Moser studied the neural processes that happen in our brains when we make mistakes and observed that mistakes literally form new connections in our brains.[49] When we make a mistake, synapses fire; a synapse is an electrical signal that moves between parts of the brain when learning occurs.

Just look at scientists developing treatments for COVID-19. The process is filled with trial and error, small steps forward and big steps backward. Failure is not just part of learning; it is *how* we learn.

Our children spend their entire childhoods in school learning that there is one right answer and that making mistakes or getting the wrong answer is bad. But when you become a maker, you need a different mindset about making mistakes. Along with curiosity and passion and the desire to create comes a different relationship with failure.

When we teach our children to walk, we celebrate every attempt, even as they make mistakes, even as they tumble and fall. Yet when our children get older, do we continue to celebrate their attempts with the same enthusiasm and patience? Does the school system celebrate our children's attempts at learning? In a standardized, fast-moving curriculum, the kids who are celebrated are the ones whose first attempt most aligns with "what is right." The paradox is that making *multiple attempts* is how children learn.

Now is the time to start celebrating the attempts, the mistakes, the tumbles and falls. That's how real learning happens, how problem-solving happens, and how creativity happens. In a standard classroom environment, even the best-intentioned teachers do not have the time to let children test an idea, fail, and then try and try again until it succeeds. *You* can give your child that time and space. When our children do make mistakes, when they inevitably fail, don't immediately jump in to help them fix it. Mistakes and failure

Mistakes and failure enable deep learning.

enable deep learning. That's when their creative-thinking and problem-solving muscles start to spring into action, and how they cultivate true self-confidence.

(The irony, of course, is that we as parents have no choice but to give entire school systems time and space as they attempt to adapt and iterate in real time to meet the evolving needs of schooling in this pandemic. We are watching them fail, learn, and try again. Hopefully, this experience will steer schools away from the idea of one-size-fits-all answers to big problems.)

On a recent neighborhood walk, my son and I saw a boy struggling to get his kickball out of a gutter pipe that runs under his driveway. A group of children had gathered to help get it out. They built different contraptions to try and remove the ball from the drainpipe. Someone attached a flashlight to a lacrosse stick to poke it out; another child duct-taped a leaf blower to a broomstick to try to blow it out. They were plotting to send the tiniest kid inside the pipe in a full military crawl. If the parents came out and retrieved the kickball for him, there would not have been this flurry of creative problem-solving and hands-on innovation. (But they may have been horrified at the state of their leaf blower!)

MAKING IS A CHOICE—YOUR CHOICE

It's a choice to give your children the space, time, and resources to make—to make a mess, to make experiments, and to make mistakes.

Now that some of our children are returning to school in different ways—whether they're physically back in school, in a distance learning model online, or a hybrid of the two—how do we still allow the time and space for them to follow their curiosity and get hands-on? In the new normal, do we risk letting ourselves settle back into old ways? Do we risk returning to the days of keeping our children busy all the time with school, homework, and extracurricular activities? Or will we make the changes needed to preserve free time, curiosity, and more hands-on experiences?

KEY TAKEAWAYS

- Many children are accustomed to heads-down learning, but changing our mental model means exploring the possibilities of hands-on learning.

- Being hands-on can mean making or building things, going outside, taking field trips, and even using technology to *create* rather than consume.

- During the pandemic, children can experience a variety of free and low-cost virtual field trips, and individualized microlearning opportunities with teachers all over the world.

- It may be human to want things to be tidy, planned, systematic, and structured, but we need to be tolerant of and even encourage the *messiness* that comes with making.

- Children benefit from having a designated place for hands-on learning, whether it is a small closet, a corner of the garage, a folding table, or a nook behind the sofa.

- Embrace mistakes and failure—that's how learning happens.

WHAT NEXT? FIVE WAYS TO BRING THIS CHAPTER TO LIFE

- **Think:** Do you encourage your children to make things, why or why not? Think about materials and resources you already have that might help your child get hands-on. For example, could your child cook a meal, build a contraption with items from the recycle bin, or sketch out an invention on a piece of paper? What could you and your child do together that is hands-on?

- **Feel:** How do you feel about messes in your home? Do you feel differently about a dirty mess, a cluttered mess, and a creative mess? What do you define as an acceptable creative mess that comes with making and building? Talk to your children about how you feel and specify the kinds of messes you will allow in the house.

- **Do:** See Appendix IV for ideas on how to make a low or no cost "back room" for your child. All you will need is an understanding of what your child wants to make, basic materials, an accessible space or table, willingness to give them autonomy to experiment, and some good old-fashioned encouragement.

- **Act:** Take a real or virtual field trip. Whether it's a trip to the local grocery store, park, or your own backyard, get into the real world and see and experience new things. Or explore any number of virtual destinations. Either way, point out interesting details, ask questions, and encourage your child to get hands-on.

- **Discuss:** Talk with your children about the things that excite them or spark their curiosity, then brainstorm how to get hands-on with those interests. Discuss what kinds of materials they might need, how they will start the process of making, and what they hope to learn.

PERSONAL CHECK-IN:
WHAT ARE YOU THINKING?

- What have I learned about the importance of making and hands-on experiences, inside and outside of school?

- How can I take advantage of free and accessible outdoor spaces near my home to give my child more time to explore nature?

- What can I do with the resources I already have to create hands-on learning opportunities for my child in my own home?

CREATIVITY

*You can't use up creativity. The more
you use the more you have.*

—MAYA ANGELOU

The World Economic Forum's *Future of Jobs Report 2020* predicts that creativity, innovation, and ideation will be essential skills for the workforce of tomorrow—a.k.a. our children.[50] Everyone from CEOs to scientists agree that our children need creative problem-solving skills to tackle our world's biggest challenges—including climate change, food supply, and renewable energy, to name a few. Experts call these next-gen skills the four Cs—critical thinking, creativity, collaboration, and communication—and are urging for the four Cs to be added to the traditional three "Rs" of reading, writing, and 'rithmetic.

Even though everyone from the *Fortune* 500 companies to the US Small Business Administration has been calling for creativity in education for years, things are changing oh-so-sloooowly. As we progress along this journey of Wonders, it is not surprising to understand why. We have learned that creativity is ignited by curiosity, which is sparked by free time to play, explore, be bored, overcome boredom, fail, overcome failure—and do it all over again. As this chapter will detail, creativity is stifled by standardization, evaluation, and pressure to conform to the structure of the school system. Our educational system "teaches to the test," which is a colloquial term for a method of education where curriculum is heavily focused on preparing students for standardized tests. This approach reinforces that there is just one correct answer to every question and one correct solution to every problem.

But all of that is changing. Why? Because living through the pandemic is proving to our children that creativity and innovation are needed. They have seen stores and restaurants adapt to changing conditions by offering curbside pickup and social distancing. They may have interacted with a pediatrician through a virtual visit on a computer or mobile phone. Many kids watched their parents adapt to a new way of remote working. These things make an impression on our children showing them that creativity enables us to adapt and solve real problems.

Creativity enables us to adapt and solve real problems.

If your children are older, they might have heard CDC experts provide guidance on how to stay safe, reverse that guidance, and then openly admit that they don't know the answers. They might see frontline medical workers improving upon treatments—learning, unlearning, and relearning—to find a better way. Our children are watching in real time as scientists track new strains of COVID-19 and try to innovate treatments as the virus itself adapts and changes. Every day, our children hear about discoveries, mistakes, successes, and failures. They are literally seeing creativity-in-process everywhere.

THE LIFESAVING POWER OF CREATIVITY

I am an emphatic believer that creativity belongs in every discipline. Let me share a very personal example that helps to explain why.

My middle son was born with craniosynostosis, a condition that occurs in one out of every two thousand live births. The condition causes premature closure of the skull bones. Most infants are born with skull bones that are "floating," which allows for the skull to compress during childbirth, and to allow for rapid brain growth during the early years of life. The edges of the skull bones, called sutures, normally close up when toddlers are between two and three years old. When a child has craniosynostosis, one or more of these sutures prematurely close, sometimes in utero. Surgery is required to open prematurely closed sutures to make room for rapid brain growth experienced by babies and relieve any pressure inside the skull.

Our pediatrician discovered the condition when my son was four weeks old. We were referred to a pediatric neurosurgeon to determine a course of action. We consulted with one of the nation's leading surgical teams, who offered "gold standard" care at Children's National Medical Center. They advised an open surgery called the Pi procedure in which the surgeon makes a large π-shaped incision in the scalp and skull to open the closed suture and then reshapes the head.

When the surgeon described this to me, he demonstrated how he would "peel back" my son's scalp and drill into his skull so he could remove the closed suture and reshape the bone before putting everything back in place with metal plates and screws. He told us that the surgery usually required multiple blood transfusions and up to two weeks in the neonatal intensive care unit. After the consultation, before he left the room, he added that the Pi procedure is generally a one-time surgery, but in complex cases, multiple surgeries might be required.

He walked out, and I remember having no words, only tears and a deep sense of fear and dread. I could not imagine putting the tiny newborn in my arms through that procedure. With the sophistication of modern medicine, how could this be the "gold standard" of care?

In the days that followed, I spoke with surgeons at other leading pediatric hospitals. Their recommendations were the same.

Finally, I discovered a doctor in San Antonio who treated craniosynostosis with an innovative procedure. He pioneered an endoscopic surgery as an alternative to the Pi procedure. It was a minimally invasive operation that took less than two hours. The surgery required just two small incisions, a one-night hospital stay, and no blood transfusions. It sounded too good to be true, but we flew to San Antonio as quickly as possible to find out.

We arrived at his humble office, where many patients crowded in the waiting room. The doctor consulted with us for almost an hour and showed before-and-after pictures of children who had benefited from his surgery. He answered our questions in detail, using models and diagrams to explain exactly what he would do when performing his innovative procedure. He showed us the surgical tools he would use on our newborn son's delicate skull and the small blue box where he would put a lock of his shaven hair to be saved as his first haircut.

I asked this doctor why other renowned hospitals did not offer endoscopic surgery as an alternative. He explained, with frustration, that medical schools are slow to adopt new surgical methods. They want to conform to best practices and industry standards and are reluctant to take risks and try new things. To accelerate the pace of learning, he was teaching workshops to other doctors to train them in his new, innovative method for treating this condition. He did not want children to unnecessarily suffer because the medical community was slow to adopt a better way.

We booked my son's surgery that day. Just a few weeks later, we flew back to San Antonio, where my son was in the operating room for forty-two minutes and lost less than a teaspoon of blood. He recovered in the hospital for eighteen hours, and we were back in our hotel room the next day. Incredibly, he needed only Tylenol for the pain.

Postsurgery, my son wore a plastic helmet for eighteen months. Today, you would never know he had surgery on his skull as a newborn.

For years, I followed this doctor and his innovative procedure. He shared his knowledge in workshops and tracked patient outcomes on his website. Yet it took almost a decade before other hospitals started offering the endoscopic alternative.

Had it not been for the creativity of this doctor to learn, unlearn, and relearn a better way, pediatric hospitals might still offer no alternative to the traditional, decades-old craniosynostosis procedure. Thousands of lives have been improved because this doctor chose creativity over conformity in the sciences.

RIGHT NOW, CREATIVITY *IS* EVERYWHERE

My experience with the surgeon and my son is a very personal example of creativity—but in fact we have witnessed equally dramatic examples of creativity thanks to the pandemic.

Our children have seen creative companies adapting in real time to meet the needs of this global health crisis. Distilleries ceased alcohol production and started making hand sanitizer. Dyson started making ventilators instead of vacuums. Bauer started making face shields instead of hockey gear. People tore up old T-shirts to make masks at home for friends, family, and frontline workers. When I participated in *The Call to Unite* broadcast, my contribution highlighted this worldwide explosion of creativity and its positive impact on humanity. You can view the video on my website at **www.emilygreene.com**.

More than ever, the world is relying on creative people. Our children see moms and dads adapt to working from home, use laundry detergent jugs as weights for exercise, make rice a thousand ways, and find a way to make ten dollars stretch into a hundred dollars without a paycheck for weeks.

This is life-changing for our children. They are witnessing people of all disciplines coming together, collaborating, learning in real time, solving problems, making mistakes—big ones, on the public stage—unlearning, relearning, and moving forward. Our children are literally *seeing* creativity transform the world,

Our children are literally *seeing* creativity transform the world.

and it is completely debunking the notion that creativity is some mysterious, elusive pixie dust that belongs in the art room.

Could it be that this global creative renaissance is provoking our children to reconsider their own creativity? I believe the answer is yes. As our children figure out how to fill their free time; follow their curiosity; start making, doing, and getting hands-on, they discover that they have the innate ability to think creatively. Being surrounded by these real-life examples offers a road map for how creativity can infuse every area of their life—not just "artistic" activities.

But there is also another factor driving the increase in creativity: simply not being in school, which all too often stifles creativity. In her book *Unlocked: Assessment as the Key to Everyday Creativity in the Classroom*, author and educator Katie White explains that there are four distinct stages students move through as part of the creative process: exploration, elaboration, expression, and reflection and response. The problem is that the structure and pace of the school day does not support students moving through all the phases and they often need more time.[51]

In a follow up interview on EdSurge, White explains this further:[52]

You have to provide physical space, emotional space, and time for kids to try things and experience either success or failure. In a school environment, we're often marching through a very content-heavy and skill-heavy curricula, which makes teachers feel pressured to move through things as quickly as possible. You might go through the exploration, where children are invited to generate their own questions, but then they don't get the chance to fully search for answers and experiment and experience the creative process. We rush to the answer too quickly. Or maybe they have a chance to do some exploration and elaboration, but there isn't enough time for them to express and share their work with meaningful audiences. Often their expression is in the form of handing something in to the teacher.

Outside of the school building with more free time, kids have more space to consciously and unconsciously work through these phases. Equally important, kids also have more time for reflection. White says: "The stage that gets most short-shrifted is reflection and response. Because this is how teachers and kids can connect their creative personality, and who they're becoming as creative individuals. They can connect past tasks to future tasks and future creative endeavors. We rarely have the time to do that reflection. The biggest enemy of creativity is time."

BREAKING OUT OF CONFORMITY
IN OUR HOMESCHOOL YEAR

Do schools completely kill creativity, as the late Ken Robinson says in his TED Talk of the same name?[53]

Never. It's not possible. Creativity is too powerful to be crushed by four walls of industrial-age thinking. However, the *conformity* required at school *smothers* creativity, leaving it gasping for air. If children don't have an outlet to develop creativity outside of school, it deteriorates.

In our homeschool year, we aimed to choose creativity over conformity. It started with an old-fashioned story time. Everyone gathered around for a read-aloud of the children's picture book called *The Big Orange Splot*, by Daniel Manus Pinkwater.

The main character, Mr. Plumbean, lives on a "neat street" where all the houses look the same. A bird flies over his house and drops a can of bright-orange paint on his roof, leaving behind an unsightly orange splot. Instead of repainting his house to look like all the others, Mr. Plumbean breaks away from conformity and paints his house in a colorful way that represent his dreams. His neighbors are appalled, thinking that something must be wrong with Mr. Plumbean. But as the neighbors talk with him, one by one, they begin to embrace his idea of creative self-expression. Eventually, Mr. Plumbean's neighbors realize that being different allows them to realize their own individuality (something we will talk about more in chapter 6).

After reading the book, we talked about conformity versus individuality. Then, the children used magazines, pictures, and drawings to create individual collages that represented all the ways they felt they had to conform in school. Through this activity, we learned so many things I didn't know about the forces of conformity in their lives.

In our discussions, the boys identified conformity as following along with what other people say and doing the same thing over and over without question. When I asked them about the monotony, they explained that it got stale hearing only their teacher's point of view. They also disliked that school forced them to learn things they didn't care about, but they had no choice in what they wanted to learn. They voiced frustration that they were expected to complete their work in a specific way and discouraged from presenting unique perspectives or creative alternatives.

HOW SCHOOLS VALUE CONFORMITY OVER CREATIVITY

The sad truth is that our school system encourages, fosters, and rewards conformity. Children are expected to line up, be quiet, sit down in rows, do what they are told, get the right answers, not question authority, and stay on track. They are expected to memorize and repeat standardized curriculum, and they are tested, graded, and evaluated based on how well their performance compares to other children their age. To keep the assembly line moving, they are discouraged from thinking, feeling, or doing anything that does not conform. School as a system values conformity, not creativity.

In school, children usually learn that creativity only belongs in certain subjects. Art, music, and theater students are expected to be creative, while other more traditional subjects do not outwardly value creative thinking. Traditional schooling reinforces the stereotype that creativity is only an artistic add-on. It's the glitter on the poster, the detail on

Traditional schooling reinforces the stereotype that creativity is only an artistic add-on.

the drawing, and the clever title of the story. For this reason, children often believe in the myth that creativity belongs only in the arts, and there is no use for creativity in other subjects like math and science. Let me be clear: there are extraordinary teachers who do value creativity in every subject, and to them we owe tremendous gratitude. My older sons had a biology teacher like this in high school who went out of her way to give students every opportunity to infuse creativity into their learning through original projects. Unfortunately, this is not common.

Parents and children also learn to self-define as either left or right-brained, with "left-brained" people leaning more toward logic and "right-brained" people leaning more toward creativity. But this well-ingrained idea is based on outdated science. In fact, brain scans clearly show that people generally use both sides of their brain equally.[54] Creativity and logic can easily coexist—yet schools perpetuate the myth that they are mutually exclusive.

> **Creativity and logic can easily coexist—yet schools perpetuate the myth that they are mutually exclusive.**

But it's not just schools' outdated definition of creativity that creates conformity. It's the structure of school itself. Conformity happens just by the nature of sitting in a classroom with other children, and with a teacher evaluating your child in relation to those other children. In the classroom, children sit next to their peers and are judged on the exact same activity with the exact same parameters. Children are naturally going to look at the people sitting next to them and say, "I should do exactly what they're doing." But all this conformity is having a scary impact.

I was devastated to read Kyung Hee Kim's research that documents a continuous decline in creativity among American schoolchildren over the last three decades.[55] People like Sir Ken Robinson captured public attention with several TED Talks on this topic—but Kim's research was the cold, hard proof.

Kim, a professor of education at the College of William and Mary, analyzed scores on the Torrance Tests of Creative Thinking (TTCT), which were collected from children grades K–12 over the course of several decades. Kim found that the scores for all grade levels have been declining since the late 1980s. A thirty-year downward trend is pretty alarming!

In Kim's words, "Children have become less emotionally expressive, less energetic, less talkative and verbally expressive, less humorous, less imaginative, less unconventional, less lively and passionate, less perceptive, less apt to connect seemingly irrelevant things, less synthesizing, and less likely to see things from a different angle."[56]

According to Kim's research, all aspects of creativity have declined, but the biggest decline is in the measure called creative elaboration, which assesses the ability to take a particular idea and expand on it in an interesting and novel way.[57] Kim herself calls it the "creativity crisis."

This creativity crisis is part of what we aimed to overcome in our homeschool year—which meant confronting some of the most deeply ingrained parts of "school": homework, tests, and grades.

THE WORST FACTOR IN CONFORMITY: HOMEWORK

My children identified homework as the worst factor in conformity—not because it was always hard, but because it brought the conformist attitudes of school into their own home, where they wanted to be free to express themselves creatively. Until that point, I had not realized how much homework impacted their creativity. Looking back, even as fourth and sixth graders, they were already drowning in homework. Their worksheets and math packets encroached upon family time, free time, play time, sports time, outside time, and just plain being-a-child time.

Even though it was more than four years ago, I clearly remember standing in front of them, trying to force them to sit down and do their math packets, when all they wanted to do was go outside and play. To me, I was helping them get their homework done before it was too late in the day. To them, I was forcing them to conform. I guess, by supporting homework, I was conforming too.

If you've felt like your children have more homework than you did, you're right. Homework has tripled in the last three decades. To what end? A 2014 study from Stanford University of 4,317 students in high-performing schools in upper-middle-class communities in California found that a majority of students identified homework as a primary source of stress, and many also reported that homework led to health issues and sleep deprivation as well as less time for friends, family, and extracurricular activities.[58]

Homework has tripled in the last three decades.

Thirty years ago, could we have predicted a psychiatric specialty in homework anxiety?

If you are raising a skeptical eyebrow on the topic of homework, you are not alone. Our ingrained beliefs about the value of homework are part of the old-school mindset that is hard to shake off. I encourage parents to read *The Homework Myth*, by Alfie Kohn, which closely examines our knee-jerk defenses of homework, including the belief that it promotes higher achievement, reinforces learning, and builds study skills and responsibility.[59] In his book, Kohn conducts an in-depth comparative analysis of studies on or pertaining to homework, learning, and academic performance. He reveals the limitations and blind spots of how studies were conducted. In the end, he concludes that many assumptions about homework simply do not pass the test of research, logic, or experience. According to his analysis, no evidence exists to support the practice of assigning homework to elementary school students. Inconsistent evidence shows an extremely low correlation between homework and achievement for students in grades six through nine, and a meaningful correlation between homework and achievement only appears above grade ten.

Interestingly, according to Kohn, "Quite a number of educators will tell you that excessive homework has been brought about to a very large extent by parental pressure." He goes on to say, "What seems to be more common, though, is a simple desire on the part of the parent for their children to succeed academically, accompanied by the belief that homework is a critical means to that end." Kohn argues that a competitive dynamic may explain why parents feel trapped in the homework cycle. He says, "Parents may feel in their hearts that their children have too much homework, but as long as everyone else is doing it, there's pressure to do it."

This may be why the internet exploded when a teacher in Texas had the courage to set a no-homework policy for her second-grade classroom.[60] She passed out a letter to every parent at a "Meet the Teacher Night" before the start of the school year to explain her no-homework policy. An overjoyed parent posted a photo of the letter on Facebook, and it went viral with over fifty-nine thousand shares. "There will be no formally assigned homework this year," the teacher explained in the letter. "Rather, I ask you spend your evenings doing things that are proven to correlate with student success. Eat dinner as a family, read together, play outside, and get your child to bed early."

This teacher said homework just was not working for her classroom anymore. So she decided to make meaningful change. She put aside the so-called ten-minute rule, which recommends ten minutes of homework per grade level per night. She had the guts to be a nonconformist and stand up to homework, and her story inspired many to do the same.

One of my biggest joys during the homeschooling year is that by choosing creativity over conformity, we left homework in the dust and never looked back.

But we still had to contend with the other elephant in the room: grades.

GETTING RID—GASP!—OF GRADES

Most students learn that their job in school is to earn good grades and high test scores by getting the correct answers. They learn by experience that creativity is not what helps them pass tests. In fact, tests and grades are big creativity killers.

Tests and grades are big creativity killers.

That's why, in our homeschool year, we not only abolished homework but tests and grades as well. To foster an environment of creativity, I needed to send a big message that grades and tests would not be important in our wondrous place of learning.

I thought a funny way to do this would be to create a spoof test, inspired by the work of Carol Dweck, a professor of psychology at Stanford University who studies motivation and how to foster success. In her book *Growth Mindset,* Dweck describes an experiment in which her team showed fifth graders a closed cardboard box and told them it had a test inside that measured an important school ability. Then, she asked the children two important questions: if they believed the test in the box could measure how smart they are, and if they believed the test in the box could measure how smart they would be when they grow up. She learned that students with a *growth* mindset did not believe the test could measure how smart they were and could not predict how smart they would be when they grew up. But students with a *fixed* mindset believed that the unseen test could measure both how smart they were and also how smart they would be when they grew up.[61]

I wondered what my own children believed. I sat the older boys at the kitchen table with number-two pencils and told them they were about to take the most important test of the homeschool year and that it could determine their performance for the rest of their lives. I slipped this fifteen-question test in front of them:

WHAT CAN GRADES MEASURE?

Mark which are true for you and which are false.

Grades measure your intelligence.	☐ True	☐ False
Grades measure your talent.	☐ True	☐ False
Grades measure your curiosity.	☐ True	☐ False
Grades measure your passion.	☐ True	☐ False
Grades measure your skills.	☐ True	☐ False
Grades measure your aptitude.	☐ True	☐ False
Grades measure your character.	☐ True	☐ False
Grades measure your creativity.	☐ True	☐ False

Grades measure your effort.	☐ True	☐ False
Grades measure your resourcefulness.	☐ True	☐ False
Grades measure your problem-solving skills.	☐ True	☐ False
Grades determine your future college.	☐ True	☐ False
Grades determine your future job.	☐ True	☐ False
Grades determine your future success.	☐ True	☐ False
Grades determine your future happiness.	☐ True	☐ False

The test was a joke, but as I watched them read each question and carefully think about which answer to choose, I realized with terror that they did not understand the joke. This single exercise, meant to lightheartedly poke fun at the limitations of grades and tests, actually revealed what my children had been taught to believe at school. They thought grades were very, very important and could predict the future of their success and learning.

Both children answered "true" for at least five of the questions. At such a young age, they placed so much value on grades. Could I blame school, or was it partly my fault? After all, the value of grades had been deeply instilled in me as a child, too.

GOOD GRADES DO NOT ALWAYS EQUAL GOOD STUDENTS

When I was in high school, I had a lot of freedom and autonomy. My parents allowed me to drive at a young age and camp in the wilderness for days at a time before cell phones were invented. They even gave me a written power of attorney to handle my own disciplinary matters at school. In contrast to this, or perhaps because of this, they set high expectations for my academic performance.

My mother grew up in Argentina in a time of political turmoil, and she was forced to leave school at a young age to work and support her family. I watched her put herself through college in my elementary years. My father grew up in a small town in Colorado with limited opportunities for educational advancement beyond the local college. At home, he read constantly and introduced us to big ideas, provoked intellectual debates, and challenged my brother and me to learn everything that was available to us.

I had a special arrangement with my parents regarding grades. If I achieved a 4.0 each semester, I had no curfew. My parents believed in the philosophy of "high freedom, high responsibility," which meant that I could earn freedom by demonstrating responsibility. However, my teenage brain distorted this idea to mean that if I took basic responsibility for getting good grades, I would have total freedom— no curfew, no restrictions, and no rules.

Good grades were my ticket to teenage freedom, and I was eager to fulfill my end of the bargain. Knowing this, you might think I was the stereotypical straight-A student and high achiever, the type of child who worked diligently, took notes, met one-on-one with teachers, studied with discipline, and worked tirelessly to go above and beyond on all my assignments to earn the highest grade.

Nope.

I wish I could say I was that kind of student in high school, but it's not true. My goal was to get good grades, not to be a good student. Sadly, at the time, I didn't understand the difference. I put forth the level of effort needed to get an A in each class, and that's all. I'm embarrassed to admit it, but I took great satisfaction in getting straight As with minimal effort. Looking back, I realize I rarely put forth extra effort unless I was inspired by an awesome teacher or was doing something I truly loved (as we talked about in chapter 3).

By my memory, it wasn't too hard to get good grades at my high school. We had fewer AP and honors classes, less homework, and more free time. While I didn't graduate with a 4.0, I did earn a solid grade point average, which gave me confidence to apply to a good university. Encouraged by good scores on the SAT and ACT, I applied early decision to my top school and was accepted, which reinforced my belief that grades and scores paved the way for future success.

That was great ... until I got to college and experienced a rude awakening.

Within my first few weeks at Northwestern, I learned that the level of effort that got me through high school would not be enough to get me through college. I noticed that other students took learning more seriously. They took notes, asked questions, met with teachers during office hours, went to the library, and checked out extra books. They studied every day, sought feedback on rough drafts, and formed peer study groups. They put enormous effort into learning. I had always skated by doing the minimum needed to get the A without any extra effort. So I stuck with my old ways and thought everything would turn out just fine.

The first semester was tough. I was overwhelmed with homework, so I relied on shortcuts to get it done. In a blink of an eye, I was taking midterm exams, and then came midterm grades. And for the first time in my life, my grades were below average.

Over the next few years at college, I ate some humble pie. I learned that what I thought was good work was average, and what I thought was great work was just good. I had to reach deep and wide out of my comfort zone to develop an understanding of what was excellent. I struggled, I resisted, and I complained. I wanted to quit, transfer, and drop out. My parents challenged me to dig deeper beyond the school experience and find my heart's connection to learning.

While I entered college as a radio, television, and film major, I questioned if that was the right path. I took a hard look at myself to figure out what really motivated me, to connect with my true passions. I explored neuroscience, Italian, and stand-up comedy. I stopped thinking about grades and started thinking about what lit me up inside. I became curious, excited, passionate, and engaged. Finally, I fell in love with learning. When the grades stopped mattering is when they started to get better.

I vowed to teach my children this important lesson: to aim for the learning not the grades. But from the moment my children started going to school, I expected them to get good grades! Why? It's that insidious old-school mental model rearing its ugly head again.

From elementary school on, we teach our children to work hard to earn good grades. Even if we don't implicitly say these words, we reinforce the idea that grades define their achievement, abilities, and potential. For many, this creates a pressure for students to perform at a high level, and grades become the ultimate measure of that performance.

The truth is, grades tell you almost nothing about your child's achievements, abilities, or potential.

But the truth is, grades tell you almost nothing about your child's achievements, abilities, or potential.

I don't blame my parents for my lazy approach to getting good grades in high school. They were trying to set high expectations for me to do well in school, and it was I who chose to put forth the minimal effort necessary to reach their expectations. They aimed to teach me that taking responsibility for my own success would grant me the freedom to make my own life choices. Eventually, I learned the lesson.

WHERE DO LETTER GRADES COME FROM?

With millions of students and parents obsessed with grades, did you ever wonder where the letter grading system came from? Like our education system, grades came with industrialization.

Long before grades, for thousands of years, students learned from mentors or masters. As apprentices, the quality of a student's education depended on the accomplishment of the teacher. Only in the last few hundred years has learning moved away from one-on-one instruction to more formal schooling. Until the eighteenth century, there was no standardized means of evaluating students and no universal measure by which students at one school were compared with students at another school.

Then in the nineteenth century, American universities experimented with different types of alpha numeric grading.[62] Yale tried a four-point scale, switched to a nine-point scale, and then reverted back to a four-point scale in 1832. Harvard first tried a numeric scale, switched to letter grades in 1883, and then switched to a rating system using labels like Class I, II, III, and IV. In 1897, Mount Holyoke College implemented a letter grade system like what is used today. By the turn of the century, grading on a one hundred-point scale became the norm until the 1940s, when letter grading gained popularity.

Letter grades depersonalized the student-teacher feedback loop. Within a generation, learning transformed from a discourse-rich experience to a letter on a piece of paper.

THE LIMITS OF GRADES

What can you actually learn about your child from their grades? Let me offer *you* a spoof test, like I did for my children.

WHAT CAN YOUR CHILD'S GRADES MEASURE?

Mark which are true for you and which are false.

How well your child performs on assessments.	☐ True	☐ False
How well your child follows directions and rules.	☐ True	☐ False
How well your child meets teachers' standards.	☐ True	☐ False
Your child's talent.	☐ True	☐ False
Your child's curiosity.	☐ True	☐ False
Your child's character.	☐ True	☐ False
Your child's emotional intelligence.	☐ True	☐ False
Your child's resourcefulness.	☐ True	☐ False
Your child's leadership ability.	☐ True	☐ False
Your child's ability to think creatively.	☐ True	☐ False
Your child's ability to solve complex problems.	☐ True	☐ False
Your child's future success.	☐ True	☐ False
Your child's ability to find joy and happiness.	☐ True	☐ False

Your child's ability to be an entrepreneur.	☐ True	☐ False
Your child's ability to collaborate with others.	☐ True	☐ False

As you can probably guess, the answers to the first three questions are "true" and the rest—all "false." Grades tell you how well your child performs on assessments—which in many classes includes participation, attendance, and other factors that are not related to academic achievement.

Grades tell you how well your child follows directions and rules. Did they cite only ten sources, and no more, no fewer? Was their presentation exactly between four to six minutes? Did they show every step of their computation work in the margin? These things show the ability to check the boxes, not to think outside of them.

Grades tell you how well your child meets teachers' standards. Does this teacher like or dislike figurative language? Does she have more appreciation for graphs and stats than testimonies or case studies? Does he favor certain views of the world as the right answer? Teachers are people; like it or not, they have biases and beliefs that influence their interactions with and assessments of your children.

But grades do not—and cannot—measure the qualities in questions four through fifteen.

GRADES STIFLE CREATIVITY—AND THEREFORE STIFLE TRUE LEARNING

Grades are like the MPAA's rating system for movies. A PG or R rating will tell you something about the content of the movie, but it won't tell you anything about the plot, the style, or, most importantly, the quality of the movie. Now, imagine if we only assessed movies based on their MPAA rating. That wouldn't be a very accurate way of evaluating whether a movie is truly good or not, would it? Likewise, grades don't tell you anything about the quality of your child's learning.

Yet we keep chasing this holy grail of grades and tests because these are the established metrics for entrance into college. Children who are highly motivated to get into the college of their dreams are encouraged to double down on better grades and test scores. This is why far too many students today will do whatever it takes to get good grades, even if that means sacrificing health, sleep, happiness, ethics, behavior—or true learning. Moreover, school systems are doing whatever it takes to ensure more children get good grades, including eliminating finals, rounding up, and implementing widespread grade inflations.

In 2018, the *Washington Post* published an article exposing widespread grade inflation in Montgomery County, Maryland.[63] The article revealed a dramatic increase in students receiving As in English, science, and Advanced Placement classes. Specifically, the number of students receiving As in math nearly doubled. At the same time, the number of students receiving Cs, Ds, and Es sharply declined.

According to the article, the surge in As came after the school system made controversial changes to how teachers evaluate students. The grading policy changed to an averaging system that allowed for final grades to be rounded up, and the school system eliminated end-of-year final exams. This type of grade inflation is not unique to Montgomery County, Maryland. It might be happening in your school system too. All this is happening in our educational system because grades are considered the be-all and end-all of learning and the golden ticket to a successful life in college and beyond. The longer we hold onto grades as the ultimate measure of our children's learning, the more we limit their creativity.

While parents and high school students spend years obsessing about grades, many colleges and universities are losing interest in grades. Admissions teams at some of the nation's most selective colleges say they barely look at an applicant's GPA. Schools are reevaluating their admission processes to come up with a better way to evaluate potential students. Why are they doing this? College admission teams know that grades reveal limited information about a student. This is addressed more in chapter 6.

LEARNING IS ABOUT QUESTIONS, NOT ANSWERS

The focus on tests and grades reinforces the mindset that answer-seeking *is* learning. This leads students to find quick answers using Google, Siri, or Alexa. In seconds, they have answers at their fingertips. Our children are so busy seeking answers that they seldom question the questions. They are not challenged enough to deepen the quality of their questions. In school, my children learned to pursue the quick and easy questions, not the profound questions that shape thinking, action, imagination, and possibility, while also unlocking the door to creativity.

Seeking answers is so easy in this age of instant gratification that thinking creatively feels like a chore. To some, it's not worth the effort. Children think, *I've done my job; I got the right answer. Now move on.* They treat answers like stop signs rather than launchpads for more questions. But the exponential pace of change means that today's answers are tomorrow's cobwebs.

LEARNING IS A CONSTANT WORK IN PROGRESS

True learning is never ending. But the process of testing and grading enforces the mindset that once you've found the right answer and received a good grade, learning on that subject is complete, and it's time to move on. This kind of "checkbox" thinking allows teachers to keep moving through lesson plans and keep students on track to complete the scope and sequence. I call it the "Grade it; move on" mindset.

Get the answer right on the test. Get a good grade. Move on.

Memorize these spelling words. Take a test. Grade it. Move on.

Do twenty math problems. Take a test. Grade it. Move on.

Write an essay. Proofread it. Grade it. Move on.

I did not realize how deeply this "Grade it; move on" mentality was ingrained in my children's approach to learning. During the first few weeks of homeschooling, my children would finish an assignment and ask me to grade it. Without the "Grade it; move on" process, the work never felt done.

So we leaned into a new idea that it's OK if the work is open-ended. All work can exist in a state of reflection and revision until the kids felt they maxed out the learning for that specific piece of work. We introduced reflection through talking, journaling, and ideation. I gave the children permission to reflect on their work, talk about it, revisit it, revise it, and continue to make changes if they felt like it was improving—as many times as they wanted to do it. This allowed them to think outside the box, to try new things, and get creative with how they wanted to explore and learn. There may come a time in their adult lives when they face deadlines and work pressures that limit the time they have to reflect on and revise their mistakes, but at least they will know how to do it.

They came to understand that learning is a work in progress, and this breakthrough enabled them to create work they did not know they were capable of when they were in a traditional "Grade it; move on" environment.

LEARNING IS NONLINEAR

Not only is true learning a constant work in progress, but it also does not move in a straight line. In school, learning is treated as linear: learn, master, move on. Rarely are children allowed to iterate on their own schoolwork. Except for essays, which usually go through a round of revisions, children are not accustomed to examining and learning from their mistakes to improve.

Real learning is not linear. Real learning is ongoing and iterative: learn, unlearn, learn again.

Real learning is not linear. Real learning is ongoing and iterative: learn, unlearn, learn again. We talked about Buckminster Fuller's Knowledge Doubling Curve in chapter 3, and how today human knowledge doubles every twelve months, and soon to be every twelve hours. What we learn today, we may well have to unlearn and relearn next year, as humanity gains new knowledge.

In the pandemic, we have watched this happen even more quickly than Fuller's curve. At first scientists concluded that the virus was passed largely through surface contact. Later, they learned that it passes mostly through airborne droplets. We are constantly learning more about the effects of the virus on the body. Even the highest-level experts, the Dr. Faucis of the world, are learning, unlearning, and relearning.

Imagine if we told the scientists working on the COVID-19 vaccine that they only got one shot (no pun intended) to make the vaccines, get graded on it, and move on—no revisions allowed! Imagine if we gave them an F if it didn't work on the first try. The idea is lunacy. We would not find a working vaccine without trial and error. The process requires learning, trying, failing, unlearning, relearning, trying again, failing again, unlearning again, relearning again, and thinking creatively until they can solve the complex problems and find the best solutions. Why wouldn't we give our children the same opportunity? As Samuel Beckett originally published in his short piece of prose entitled *Worstward Ho*, "Ever tried. Ever failed. No matter. Try again. Fail again. Fail better."

LEARNING REQUIRES CREATIVITY, NOT CONFORMITY

True learning—nonlinear, ongoing, and focused on questions and not answers—requires creativity, not conformity.

As part of my academic work, I studied the work of E. Paul Torrance, a pioneer for more than fifty years in creativity research and education. He advocated for creativity in education and conducted extensive research on how to teach creativity to children.

In our homeschool year, I wanted to use the work of Torrance to replace the "Grade it; move on" mentality. I wanted to challenge my children to flex their *creativity* muscles instead of conforming to the standard measures of success in school. My goal was to help them increase their creative fluency, flexibility, originality, and elaboration, by giving them plenty of opportunities to be creative every day. That's why we removed grades and tests from the equation.

Without grades and tests, guess what happened? Suddenly, the fear of failure disappeared! The boys did not worry about "performing well" because there was no fixed definition of what performing well meant. Instead of calling projects that didn't work failures, we called them experiments. For example, we tried to use gumdrops, Twizzlers, and toothpicks to build an edible model of DNA. Our gumdrop "nucleotides" were too soft and heavy to attach to the Twizzler "backbone" so we ended up with a gooey mess. Even though it didn't turn out as planned, the kids still learned that Adenine-Thymine and Cytosine-Guanine are always paired together in the double helix.

We also didn't use the terms *deadline* or *due date*; we removed all sense of artificial time pressure that results from the standard scope and sequence. We silenced our inner critics so that we could exercise our creativity without fear of judgment, from ourselves or others. We challenged each other to not conform, to stay true to our individuality, and to take brave steps on our own creative journeys.

We explored what creativity is and the many ways in which it can appear. Using activities from the Kiddovate program, we talked about creative thinking, creative expression, and creative output. We brainstormed how people across all kinds of professions might show creativity in their work, now and in the future. This visionary thinking inspired my children, so we carried it from the kitchen table to Odyssey of the Mind team practice.

A typical Odyssey of the Mind practice begins with a spontaneous creative-thinking challenge. That week, I asked the teams to share what they wanted to be when they grew up. Their responses included things like football player, dancer, engineer, actor, teacher, pilot, scientist, lawyer, veterinarian, environmentalist, game developer, and stuntman.

Then I set a few unexpected prompts on the table and invited the kids to take a look. I printed out pictures of an Oculus virtual reality headset, a 23andMe genetic testing kit, a 3-D limb printer, and a sensing skull cap that kids wear under a sports helmet to detect head impact. I also set out a robot action figure, an iPhone, a laser pointer, a toothbrush, a bottle of vitamins, a toy drone, and a hearing aid. The kids investigated the items for ten minutes. I encouraged them to imagine how any of these things might be used in the jobs of tomorrow.

Then, I gave each team five minutes to imagine a popular job that might exist in the year 2025, and in the year 2035. This is what they said.

CREATIVE JOBS OF THE FUTURE

JOBS OF 2025	JOBS OF 2035
Genetic artist	Drone control center dispatcher
Programmer for robotic policemen	3D food-printer engineer
Travel agent for virtual reality vacations	Robotic lobbyist
Free time specialist	Extra memory implanter
Interactive video game designer	Technological athlete enhancer
Robotic and AI teachers and babysitters	Weather control expert
Fashion designer for athletic performance monitoring clothes	Space tour guide
Personalized 3-D bicycle manufacturer	Human organ designer
Automated dog walkers	AI brain implantation specialist
Virtual reality national park ranger	Contact sports avoidance referee
Clean water developer	Air recyclers
Trash engineer	Solar-powered food expert

It took several months, but finally, my children stopped seeing creativity as a poster or an art project. They started to see creativity as an expression of their own thinking, through talents, interests, passions, and skills. They began to self-identify as creative people, and your children can do the same. As our children see and appreciate the creative qualities in themselves, they began to take their own creative risks in self-expression.

THE FUTURE IS CREATIVITY— AND THE FUTURE IS NOW

There have been innumerable books written and talks given about how the creative economy is the future, and how the American education system is not preparing our children for that future. It has been beaten into our heads that our children need to be creative thinkers and problem-solvers. But the education system has not budged. It's stuck in the mud.

Well, now is our chance to put our children's creativity in an incubator and nourish it, because the minute they go back into the school building, creativity is in danger of being smothered again.

This is an opportunity for your child to recenter themselves around the idea that they were born creative. They have the opportunity to redefine themself as a creative person outside the superficial labels of school. Starting today, they can see themselves as creative thinkers, creative feelers, and creative doers. And if our children bring that sentiment back into their education, no one can strip it away from them. If we keep encouraging them to break the patterns of conformity through creativity, our children can follow their hearts, discover their passions, and step into their own *individuality*.

KEY TAKEAWAYS

- Creativity belongs everywhere, not just in the arts.

- Creativity *is* everywhere—something our children are witnessing firsthand during the pandemic.

- School, homework, and grades contribute to stifling creativity and promoting conformity.

- A grade cannot attest to or define your child's intelligence, personal strengths, or future success.

- Creativity among school-age children has declined dramatically in the past several decades.

- True learning requires creativity.

- The move away from conformity and toward creativity unlocks individuality.

WHAT NEXT? FIVE WAYS TO BRING
THIS CHAPTER TO LIFE

- **Think:** Think about your child's strengths, can all of these attributes be measured by tests, grades, and homework? Where do tests, grades, and homework fit into your deeply held beliefs about school and learning? Next time your child brings home a test or report card, how might you react differently?

- **Feel:** How do you feel about conformity versus creativity in school and in life? When you were a student, were there aspects of schooling that you did not want to conform with? How would it make you feel if your child chose creativity over conformity at the expense of a letter grade?

- **Do:** When you see or hear something creative in the world, big or small, make a point to call it out. Notice it, recognize it, and share what you think about it. Make an effort to look for and notice creativity in your child's schoolwork and other pursuits. When you see it, call it out, and praise them for it. On the flip side, call it out when you *don't* see creativity. When you see or hear something that is stale, unimaginative, outdated, or boring, call it out. Wonder out loud what might happen if that thing were reimagined through the lens of creativity. Invite your child to think about it and share creative ideas about how something might be improved.

- **Act:** Ask your kids to take the spoof test earlier in this chapter. What can you learn from their answers? Reassure your children that grades offer a very limited view of measurement and do not define them as a person.

- **Discuss:** Discuss with your family and friends how creativity shows up in your own lives—both personally and professionally. Discuss ways in which it could show up more with awareness and effort.

PERSONAL CHECK-IN:
WHAT ARE YOU THINKING?

- What is my opinion about the value of creativity in education? How is my opinion the same or different than other family members?

- Do I believe in the myth that "left-brained" people are more logical and "right-brained" people are more creative? Why or why not? What can I do to let go of this belief?

- Do I believe that creativity belongs in all subject areas and professions? Why or why not?

- How can I notice and encourage creativity in my own child, from small everyday acts of creativity to larger displays of creativity?

INDIVIDUALITY

Today you are You, that is truer than true. There is no one alive who is Youer than You.

—DR. SEUSS

One of the hardest things that children and teens face is simply figuring out who they are and what they want to become. What every parent wants, deep down, is for their child to live their most fulfilling life as their best and truest self. We all want our children to find the lifelong prize of their own *individuality*.

However, our prepandemic lives left little time for the self-reflection needed to discover individuality. Before the pandemic, our children spent around one thousand hours per year at school, participating in activities and doing homework, not counting summer and winter break. This didn't leave a lot of time to establish a sense of unique individuality.

But as we talked about in chapter 2, the pandemic loosened our schedules, and our children have experienced unprecedented amounts of free time to think about what makes them tick and what makes them happy. As adults, when they reflect back on this time in their lives, they may very well discover that their days in quarantine were when lifelong passions and interests took root and shaped the rest of their lives.

Let's not squander this opportunity to help them step into their own individuality.

FINDING YOUR CHILD'S NORTH STAR

If you worry about your child following their heart and finding purpose and passion in the world, you are not alone. Some counselors believe that parents worry too much that their children have no self-direction or definitive plans for the future. This can cause parents to put pressure on their child to pick a path, or even try to choose a path for them. But will this help or harm a child's passion?

Teens must go through the self-reflective process of asking questions like "Which colleges should I apply to?" "What major should I choose?" and "What do I want to do with my life?" As parents, we naturally want to give advice and steer them in the right direction, but it's a delicate balance, as these are choices that belong to them. To help them find their North Star, we need to encourage children of all ages to be curious about and explore different things with no strings attached.

My experience is that passion cannot be harvested unless it is planted. It's up to us as parents to encourage our children to grow into the people they are becoming. We must stay involved as they develop their individuality, expose them to a variety of things, show enthusiasm, support them as their interests change, encourage their dreams, and be their biggest fans. Often, children's interests will be different from what parents expect or desire. Even in these situations, we must help them build confidence in their own individuality. This is when passion blooms.

Passionate children truly stand out. They have a strong sense of direction about what they want to be and do as they grow up. They weave their passions into everyday life—even school. They have self-awareness, authenticity, and a desire to learn. They are more decisive and less afraid of failure. They are resilient; a minor setback will not deter them from their passion. When we see these qualities in our children, we must encourage them. As a parent, you can look for the passions that light up your child. What gets them excited, gets them out of bed, and breaks a bad mood. Notice these things—and help your child notice them too. As these passions emerge, keep note of them. It might be that they are all traceable to one common thread. Then simply mirror these things back at your child and let them connect the dots.

If you add up Wonders one through five—unlearning, free time, curiosity, making, and creativity—the conditions exist for your child's individuality to emerge like the sunshine after the rain. Each one of these Wonders feeds on and into the others in a glorious cycle, which leads your child to learn about and appreciate what makes them unique.

> **If you add up Wonders one through five, the conditions exist for your child's individuality to emerge.**

INTERSECTIONS BETWEEN TALENTS AND PASSIONS

The following fun activity comes from the Kiddovate program and encourages children to explore their individuality. To start, you will make two lists on a sheet of paper, one next to the other. At the top of the list on the left, write "Talents." At the top of the list on the right, write "Passions." Leave an open space between the two lists.

First, ask your child to write down their talents. Remind them that these are the areas in which they feel confident—whether it's sports, music, communication, leadership, friendship, a hobby, or an aspect of their personality. If they're struggling to think of their talents, ask them to consider what friends, teachers, or coaches might say about them. You can share your thoughts on their special talents too. Urge them to write at least ten talents on the list.

Next, ask your child to write down their passions. Encourage them to think about activities that make them happy. If they could do anything in their free time, what would it be? If they had unlimited resources to learn something from someone, what would they learn, and from whom? What are they most curious about? What would they want to be known for by others? What have they always dreamed of doing? What is their favorite hobby or dream hobby? What could they talk about for hours on end? Again, encourage them to write at least ten passions on the list.

Now, here is where it gets fun and creative as you show your child how to start playing with the intersections between their talents and passions. In the open space between the two lists, encourage your child to draw lines connecting different talents and passions. One by one, they will intentionally force themselves to find connections between the two. For example, if one of your child's talents is math and one of their passions is mystery novels, your child may combine these two ideas and come up with an intersection like "Write a short mystery novel using math in all the clues." Or let's say your child has a talent of making people laugh and a passion for fishing; your child may combine these two ideas and come up with an intersection of "Create your own stand-up comedy performance based on fishing jokes." There are infinite permutations for self-discovery.

TALENTS   PASSIONS

Math   *Comedy routine with fishing jokes*   Fishing

Making People Laugh   *Mystery novel with math clues*   Cooking

Singing   *Make a cookbook using cartoons*   Mystery Novels

Drawing Cartoons   *Learn to sing campfire songs*   Camping

In my experience doing this activity with hundreds of kids from all walks of life, there is usually a moment when the child starts to get excited and sees new possibilities for developing their own individuality. I encourage you to try this with your own child.

Not all of the ideas they come up with will be good, or even viable. Some might be downright silly, and that should be encouraged. The point is to get their creative gears going. Stick with it, and I assure you that some diamonds will emerge as you find where your child's passions and talents intersect.

As parents, we want our children to utilize their talents to live up to their full potential. Help your child find inspiration for their passion by drawing out as many talents and interests as you can. Foster and nurture these things as they will ultimately uncover passion—and science proves that passion (backed by skill and effort) drives success.

Researchers at the National Academy of Sciences examined the postgrad success rates of more than eleven thousand West Point students. Upon entrance to the school, students were asked to share if their motives for success were internal motives like "to become a leader in the US military," or instrumental motives including things like "to get a good job." When students were evaluated after gradua-tion, those with strong internal motives and weak instrumental motives fared better. In other words, those who had passion for their career choice succeeded, while those who wanted accolades and recogni-tion were less successful.

> **Those who had passion for their career choice succeeded, while those who wanted accolades and recognition were less successful.**

YOUR CHILD IS RETURNING TO SCHOOL; HOW DO YOU KEEP INDIVIDUALITY ALIVE?

As you encourage their passions and interests, your child is starting to get a sense of who they are outside of the walls of the school building. But in all likelihood, if they haven't already, they will soon be returning to a school environment with tests, grades, strict divisions between subject areas, standardization, and conformity. What happens when this child, whose curiosity and creativity has started blossoming, is put back into the conformity of school? How do you keep their budding individuality alive in that environment?

You can continue to protect their free time, curate their curiosity, encourage them to make and build, and foster their individuality by praising their creativity. You can also encourage them to bring these aspects of themselves back into their school system in new ways.

For example, encourage your children to bring individuality into their classes by self-advocating for choice in projects. If the teacher plans to give a multiple-choice unit test, urge your child to ask if they can make a poster, a brochure, or a podcast covering the subject matter instead. If they are uninspired by the list of writing prompts for a class paper, encourage them to ask the teacher about selecting a personalized prompt that they are more excited to write about. When they are given an assignment, encourage them to ask the teacher, "Can I make a short film for my final? Can I write a short story? Can I put on a play? Can I build a contraption that would demonstrate this principle of physics?" The worst that can happen is the teacher says no—but more often than not, teachers appreciate the initiative because they know it shows a passion for learning.

As parents, you can also help teachers come up with opportunities to integrate more individuality into Zoom-based lessons.

To inspire ideas, check out the Big List of Zoom Boosters in Appendix V.

The more you encourage your children to bring their individuality into the classroom, the more you will be setting them up for success—not just in grade school but also in college and beyond. Because the truth is, what matters out in the world is not grades or tests or a perfect GPA. What matters is individuality.

OUT IN THE WORLD, INDIVIDUALITY IS WHAT MATTERS

I recently sat in on a college recruiting seminar with recruiters from Harvard, Princeton, Yale, UVA, and other top-tier schools. All they could talk about was how every application and essay is exactly the same. There is so much conformity. A friend who sits on the board of a private university confided to me that their university actually has an ink stamp with the letters SOAAO. The admissions team presses this stamp onto the tops of applications that show individuality. The acronym means "Stands out above all others."

What makes an application stand out? It's not a 4.3 GPA or a 1600 SAT score—thousands of applications have those. What makes an application stand out above all the others is when the student knows who they are, when they have a unique identity, and when they embrace their individuality—and their actions and application show it.

Likewise, test scores only show one facet of aptitude. Since creativity and problem-solving are increasingly valued in our world, colleges and universities know they must find a way to attract students who excel in these areas. They want to see how students think, what they do, and what makes them unique.

University admissions teams know that grades and test scores cannot capture the essence of a student. They know that selecting applicants based on grades, GPAs, and standardized test scores is an imperfect system. Like us, they also want a better way. This is why some of the most well-regarded schools have stopped emphasizing standardized testing, including places like American University, Middlebury College, New York University, Wake Forest University, and, yes, Harvard. Especially during the pandemic, when many standardized tests have been cancelled, colleges and universities are being forced to develop more personalized ways of evaluating applicants.

Some of the most well-regarded schools have stopped emphasizing standardized testing.

But it's not just colleges who care more about individuality; it's also what employers want. While a small set of government, medical, and commercial jobs may require the submission of grades and transcripts with job applications, the vast majority of today's employers do not. Let's shatter the myth that future employers deeply care about your child's academic transcript. Chances are most won't even look at it because grades and test scores tend not to predict success in the workplace. Why? Because the modern workplace is absolutely nothing like school, which follows the industrial model from more than one hundred years ago.

Today, employers want to know that your child comes to the job market with the necessary skills and knowledge to be valuable in the workplace. You might be surprised to learn that this may or may not even require a college diploma! Companies like Google or Facebook do not ask applicants to submit their GPAs, test scores, or diplomas. Some of my *Fortune* 500 clients don't care if employees went to college; they only care that they have the right skills, aptitudes, and attitudes for the job.

What exactly are those skills, aptitudes, and attitudes? They want to see people who have passion and interest tied to a sense of ambition, initiative, resourcefulness, and grit. They want thinkers and doers, problem-solvers and problem-finders. They don't want test takers or box checkers, because that's not the world we live in. They want creative, curious people who can think differently and change the world.

As a business owner, I attest to this fact. Part of my role is to interview promising new talent. I love this aspect of my job because it gives me an opportunity to get to know people before we work together. When I first started interviewing candidates, I asked straightforward, run-of-the-mill questions, such as: "What are your strengths and weaknesses?" "Where do you see yourself in five years?" and "What are your top skills?"

It didn't take long to realize that standard questions got canned answers that don't reveal the uniqueness of a candidate. So I researched how people I admire conduct interviews and discovered that many of them ask unusual questions. For example, Richard Branson asks, "What didn't you put on your résumé?" Miranda Kalinowski, Facebook's global head of recruiting, asks, "On your very best day at work—the day you come home and think you have the best job in the world—what did you do that day?"

I tried asking these types of questions, and many others, all in an effort to uncover candidates' individuality. Finally, after many years, I found one very effective question: "What questions do you have for me?"

I found that many candidates are not prepared to ask unique questions. They spend their preparation time rehearsing well-practiced answers instead of thinking deeply about the job opportunity for which they are interviewing. When I ask, "What questions do you have for me?" the candidate often gets uncomfortable, shifts awkwardly, and says some version of "Oh, let me think about that." A few seconds later, some candidates admit that they have no questions. Others come up with a basic question on the spot like "Tell me more about your services" or "How long have you been in business?" I feel badly for these candidates because these superficial questions suggest superficial understanding of the job they are interviewing for and the company they claim to be excited to join.

However, occasionally I meet a candidate who lights up when I ask this question. They open their notebook, where I see a page of handwritten questions. I invite them to ask as many questions as they want because each question reveals their unique perspective and individuality. Here are some of the questions these candidates have asked:

"How do you know when something this agency creates is good enough. Isn't that subjective? Who ultimately decides?"

"How do you define a good leader at this company, and is your vision of leadership fixed or flexible?"

"Can a hardworking introvert with a can-do attitude and entrepreneurial spirit be as successful here as a hardworking extrovert?"

These are rich and complex questions that reveal the thinker underneath. Through these types of questions, we start to know each other, authentic

> **Rich and complex questions reveal the thinker underneath.**

information flows back and forth, and a real human connection is formed. This doesn't always mean that the candidate gets the job, but it often means that we have better odds of discovering if it is a mutual fit. And I will share that not once in twenty years have I ever asked about grades, transcripts, or standardized test scores.

SHOWCASING YOUR CHILD'S INDIVIDUALITY: THE PORTFOLIO

How do colleges and employers measure creativity, uniqueness, and individuality? If they aren't looking at GPAs, grades, tests, and transcripts, then what are they looking at? How can your child present who they are to the world?

As we discussed in chapter 5, there's nothing more impersonal than grades and standardized tests, yet they are the only measurement system we have in place. Parents have a hard time wrapping their heads around any other way to assess their children's progress in school—myself included. Here I am, preaching disruption, and I still find myself worrying about how my oldest son is preparing for the SAT.

But there is another way. Let me share an example. In early 2018, an aspiring copywriter made a clever video that went viral on social media. This young man's dream was to land a high-profile advertising job. He wanted to stand out, so he ditched the old-fashioned cover letter and résumé and decided to *show* his skills rather than just talk about them.

He made an original rap video[64] about the very brand he wanted to write for—Sprite. He created catchy music, clever lyrics, and visually rich special effects that brought his talent and skills to life in a way that caught the attention of the advertising industry at large. He took big creative risks like riding a hoverboard while rapping, wearing a green-and-yellow Sprite-themed suit, and falling fully clothed into a swimming pool. He became known as the "Sprite guy," and thousands of people (many of them recruiters) watched his viral video.

I was one of them. I was blown away by his passion, creativity, and willingness to show his talents. In this competitive job market, his decision to demonstrate what he can actually do and his attitude toward the job search process made him unforgettable.

What was the payoff? Besides millions of views and a prominent feature in *Adweek*, his bold move landed him the job of his dreams with the big ad agency that holds the Sprite account.

Imagine if this charismatic, funny, and energetic guy had limited his story to a résumé. On paper, his pizzazz would be reduced to a bunch of adjectives and dates. And that interview in *Adweek*?[65] It did not mention his GPA, grades, or test scores even once.

I love this story because it illustrates perfectly the new world in which we live. It doesn't matter if you child has a 4.0 from Harvard if they are unable to show what they can *do*. Today, employers want to see skills, talents, passions, interests, and proof. I interview dozens of young people every year, many fresh out of college. I have never, ever asked about their grades or test scores. I, and millions of other employers, are far more interested in how they think and what they can do.

MAKING A PORTFOLIO

In an ideal world, every child would graduate from high school with a personalized narrative that describes the essence of who they are and how they have grown throughout their schooling. This narrative report could contextualize curriculum through the lens of the learner, and include insight, recommendations, and vignettes that bring the whole student to life. With the explosion of multimedia tools, this narrative could include video, audio, and excerpts from student work. Something like this could exist, at first, in addition to grades and test scores. And eventually, instead of them.

Even better, students could participate in or lead this process by culminating their graduation with an in-depth self-reflection of their learning journey—considering the past, present, and future—leaving the graduate with a stronger sense of identity and a fuller picture of who they are.

If you find this idea unrealistic, know that grade-free high schools and universities already exist. These schools believe that their students are more intrinsically motivated learners than students at schools that emphasize the importance of grades. You might also be surprised to learn that there is a teacher-led movement to abolish grades. A leader of this movement is Mark Barnes, who "threw out grades and never looked back" after fourteen years as a classroom teacher. He founded a Facebook group called "Teachers Throwing Out Grades," which today is eleven thousand members strong. His community shares ideas, strategies, and success stories about schools and teachers that have embraced alternate forms of assessment.

A reimagining of grades is happening, with advocates inside and outside the traditional education system. The pandemic might accelerate this shift, as entire school systems have realized the limitations of traditional grading during the pandemic. For example, how can teachers equitably proctor online tests? How can students be comparatively ranked against one another when some remote learners have connectivity or technology issues? How can teachers guarantee mastery of curriculum when prepandemic teaching strategies are no longer effective? This is why some school systems have shifted to pass/fail grading during distance learning.

> **We can take steps to help our children see themselves as deep and complete beyond the gradebook.**

As we wait to see how the dust settles with grades, I believe we have an opportunity to challenge the status quo ourselves. We can take steps to help our children see themselves as deep and complete beyond the gradebook. This is why I recommend creating a portfolio for your child in addition to traditional academic transcripts, test scores, or résumés.

This is a lesson I learned during our homeschool year. We moved away from grades, yet I was legally responsible to document the boys' learning. In the state of Maryland, the umbrella organization overseeing my compliance with homeschooling laws required me to submit detailed documentation of our homeschooling experience. At first, I viewed this as a daunting administrative task—until I attended a documentation workshop led by the passionate leader of the Many Paths of Natural Learning organization. She shared sample homeschool portfolios from other parents, and I was surprised to find myself inspired. I realized creating a portfolio of learning was about more than just legal compliance, it was also about creating a keepsake that would forever remind my children of their learning, growth, and development.

I shifted my mindset to view our homeschool portfolio as an

opportunity to do what the school system could not: personalize and individualize the story of my children's learning. Rather than imagining a compliance-checker as the reader of the homeschool portfolio, I imagined that the readers would be my children as they grew up and looked back on all they had done. Still today, they enjoy looking back to see how they grew and changed as students during that year, and we have carried this portfolio mindset forward.

START CREATING A PORTFOLIO WITH YOUR CHILD

As a parent, you can encourage and help your child start the process of creating a portfolio of ongoing growth and learning. This is no time for the "Grade it; move on" mindset that we talked about in chapter 5. This is an open-ended project of self-discovery. Creating a portfolio is a project that unfolds over weeks or months—even years—and the sooner you start, the more fun it becomes. Think about how enjoyable it is when Facebook shows you an "On This Day" memory to look back on in your history. Now think of how fun and meaningful it will be for your child to have that same ability to look back on the journey of their own learning.

So what will your child's portfolio look like? The word might call to mind a big leather case holding printed pieces of creative work. That's the old vision of a portfolio. The new vision of a portfolio is a collection that captures who your child is—their story, curiosities, passions, talents, experiments, accomplishments, and areas of strength and struggle as they grow. Think of it as an organized collection of information and evidence that captures your child's individuality both in and out of school.

Some parents ask, "Who creates the portfolio, the parent or the child?" Ideally, both! When undertaking something new, our children need guidance and encouragement. During our homeschool year, I started tossing ticket stubs, written work, photographs, drawings, pictures of field trips, names of documentaries we watched, and all types of things that documented their learning in a big cardboard box. Soon, my kids followed suit. Sometimes, I would find them rummaging in the box to remind themselves of what we had done in previous months. Depending on the age of your child, the amount of parental involvement will vary. But by modeling the importance of the process, you will be teaching your child a new and vital skill of taking ownership and having autonomy for telling their own story outside the gradebook.

If you or your child has never tackled a portfolio before, don't worry; you can start now to collect things that bring your child's story to life in an exciting and personalized way. The goal of the portfolio is to show who they are, how they think, what they can do, where they want to go, and how hard they are willing to work to get there. To make a portfolio, there are two basic steps.

First, decide how you and your child will collect information, physically or digitally. Our family does both. There's nothing wrong with storing portfolio materials in an old box, like I did. Some people prefer hanging file folders or a desk tray. I suggest leaving sticky notes nearby so you and your child can make notes about specific accomplishments or reflections. Some people, especially teens, prefer digital storage. My kids snap photos of things they want to save, while I prefer to scan documents and save them on my computer. My opinion is that items saved in digital format are less easy to browse as a whole, so I favor the "old box" approach. For older children, encourage them to document favorite assignments, books or topics that inspired them, and interests or activities they enjoyed outside of school.

You will be so grateful to have saved these details when it comes time for your child to apply for internships and colleges. Also, remember that you will collect much more than you actually need, so don't worry if it feels like a lot. Think of this portfolio activity as a multidimensional progress report that considers all aspects of your child, not just grades. But, if your child also wants to document and include their grades, encourage them to include this facet of their learning.

Second, decide what format or formats will be used to create the portfolio. For a young child, this could be a scrapbook or "All About Me" book with pictures, drawings, and handwritten descriptions. For a tween, it could be a wall-mounted vision board, paper poster, or digital slideshow that captures your child's story. In the Kiddovate program, kids created portfolios in the format of notebooks, Power-Points, collages, and even original songs. Your high schooler might choose to make a video, a website, a podcast, or use an online portfolio software. There is no wrong way to make a portfolio, so let your child pick a format that excites them. For your reference, I've included what I call the WONDER method in Appendix VI.

Wondering how to go about creating a portfolio for your child? See Appendix VI.

By documenting your child's journey in progress, they will not be forced to contextualize their entire learning experience when they sit down to write college essays. As children participate in the portfolio process over time, they begin to reflect on and understand their own development. This, in turn, helps them feel responsible for the direction and outcome of their learning. When it came time for my high schooler to tell his story in applications for summer programs and internships, he appreciated easy access to things he valued along the way and was able to insightfully reflect on his own growth while also seeing opportunities for future development.

You can help your children with self-reflection by asking open-ended questions like "What can you tell me about the work you've saved? Do you see any patterns or themes? If you were to undertake that project again, would you do it differently? What were the greatest challenges in accomplishing the work you were most proud of? What does this portfolio reveal about your personal style, thought processes, and individuality? How has it helped you get to know yourself better?"

THE JOURNEY TO JOY

As you help your children create a portfolio and encourage them to pursue their passions, remember that your children are still just that: children. The journey of discovering identity is the purpose of youth, and the wonderful thing about that journey is that it's cumulative. Each new interest and each new passion builds who your child is becoming.

> **The journey of discovering identity is the purpose of youth, and the wonderful thing about that journey is that it's cumulative.**

Part of discovering individuality is your child learning how to follow the stirrings in their heart and learning how to figure out what they're passionate about.

The point is not for your child to know exactly what they want to do with the rest of their life when they're twelve years old—or even when they're eighteen years old. They may have something they're super passionate about one month; but something completely different the next month. That's part of the love of learning. The point is for them to learn how to listen to and follow their heart to joy.

When our children are young, we allow their passions and curiosities to be fluid. When my oldest son was young, he was really into trucks. Then dinosaurs. Then African animals. When he moved from one passion to the next, we didn't try to force him back to his old interests. We let him follow where his interests led. That's the natural instinct of a parent with a young child. As our children grow up through adolescence, we can lose the fluid, unconditional support for fluctuating passions and interests. We might start wanting to pigeonhole them and push them to choose the path they will follow for the rest of their life before they're even old enough to vote.

Your child may develop their lifelong soul passion when they're a teenager, but they also might not. That doesn't mean they won't have passions. Passion doesn't mean following a singular pursuit until college. Passion, like curiosity, changes.

When your child announces she's going to be a stunt pilot, let her dream a little. When she changes her mind and decides to be a chef, go with it. Track what her passions and interests are, and support the development and changes of these passions as they grow.

Childhood and teenage years are so precious when it comes to cultivating the experience of self-discovery for our children. How can they do that if they don't have the freedom to pursue who they are—including their individual interests, curiosities, and passions, as changeable as those might be?

It's not about knowing the end point; it's about the journey. We have the opportunity to let our children experience that journey in a way our educational system has not encouraged. Allowing children to pursue what they as individuals are interested in or passionate about is what rekindles our final Wonder: the brightly blazing *joy* of learning—not just throughout school, but throughout their entire lives.

KEY TAKEAWAYS

- If you combine unlearning, free time, curiosity, making, and creativity, you will nurture individuality.

- Parents who want to raise passionate children should foster their child's unique individuality—wherever it goes.

- It's essential to protect, support, and encourage your child's individuality as they return to school.

- Some colleges have deprioritized grades and test scores in favor of individuality.

- Most employers don't pay much attention (if any at all) to grades and test scores. Individuality is what matters out in the real world.

- Your child's discovery and development of their individuality is about the journey, not the destination.

WHAT NEXT? FIVE WAYS TO BRING THIS CHAPTER TO LIFE

- **Think:** Reflect on what makes your child unique. Looking back, what has fostered this uniqueness and what has stifled it? How has your child's unique individuality changed and evolved over time?

- **Feel:** Looking back at your life, what emotions do you feel about your own individuality? What has fostered your uniqueness and what has stifled it? What can you learn from this as you think about supporting your child's journey to individuality?

- **Do:** Go ahead and help your child start to build a portfolio. There are many fun and different ways to do this. See Appendix VI for one approach to try.

- **Act:** When your child receives a school assignment that is not motivating or exciting, encourage them to brainstorm a creative alternative and propose it to their teacher. Challenge them to stick with it and continue striving to bring individuality into their schoolwork.

- **Discuss:** Talk with your children about what it means to stand in individuality. Discuss how and why unique personal attributes are highly valued in the real world. Watch the "Sprite Guy" video together and discuss the plusses and minuses of this approach to individuality.

PERSONAL CHECK-IN:
WHAT ARE YOU THINKING?

- How do I think about and articulate my own individuality? Is this easy or hard? Why?

- How do I think about and articulate my child's individuality? Is this easy or hard? Why?

- How can I help my child think about and articulate their own individuality?

JOY

The beautiful thing about learning is that
nobody can take it away from you.

—B. B. KING

We've reached the final stage of our journey through the Seven Wonders of Learning. We've started to *unlearn* some deeply held and outdated beliefs about school. We've embraced a newfound *free time* and experienced how it can unlock *curiosity* in our children. We've seen how *curiosity* leads to passions and interests, more time in nature, and opportunities for *hands-on learning* and *making* things. In turn, these Wonders foster *creativity* and nourish our children's *individuality*, helping them tune in to the stirrings of their own hearts. Altogether, this journey leads us toward the *joy* of learning.

JOYLESS VERSUS JOYFUL

Before our homeschooling year, it was a chore to get my children excited about going to school. *Joy* is definitely not a word I or my children would have associated with education—a feeling I'm sure many parents share, especially those with older children. According to a report in *Critical Studies in Education*, 40 percent of US high school students have little or no interest in school.[66] It's not uncommon for a child, who spent the first years of their life learning with great delight, to lose the spark when forced to learn a standardized curriculum that they might have no interest in whatsoever.

Over time, this has an impact. There are a variety of possible outcomes: the child stays engaged and can gain interest in what is being taught; the child loses interest because they are not learning what they want to learn and don't want to learn what they are being forced to learn; or the child loses interest in learning overall.

Sadly, most children adapt to this lack of choice in learning. In the end, many just accept that they must learn what is being taught in order to succeed by status quo standard of tests and grades. Tragically, this leads many children to lose the joy of learning.

This is more than an emotional loss; it is also a physical loss. Judy Willis, MD, a board-certified neurologist and middle school teacher, specializes in the neuroscience of joyful learning. In *Psychology Today*, she writes: "Children who appear lazy, oppositional, inattentive, scattered, unmotivated, or inseparable from their social media may not be making voluntary choices. Their brains may be responding to the stress of sustained or frequent boredom."[67]

Willis is not talking about the kind of boredom that leads to free time as we discussed in chapter 2; she's talking about the mind-numbing boredom caused by burdensome memorization and test preparation for material that is uninteresting or has little relevance to children's lives. Willis continues, "Cutting edge neuroimaging research reveals significant disturbances in the brain's information processing circuits in stressful learning environments. Information communication is blocked in these stress states and new learning cannot pass into memory storage. The 'thinking, reflective' upper brain cannot downward regulate to direct behaviors, which then become involuntary."

Basically, when children learn in a joyless environment over time, their brains learn to disengage. Willis adds: "For many children, the stress response to boredom and low personal relevance builds year after year when they do not find learning interesting or relevant. When children's brains develop negativity to school, the stress state limits their voluntary control to sustain attention in class, do homework carefully, and persevere at challenging classwork."

> **When children learn in a joyless environment over time, their brains learn to disengage.**

The paradox is that the environment of traditional school is antithetical to the environment that optimizes joyful learning. It's no wonder that after years of schooling, some children believe that learning just isn't fun. The tragedy is that some of these children completely lose sight of what they are passionate about, and it is not until a midlife crisis that they try to seek it anew.

I'm sure we've all seen this midlife crisis happen to people—if we haven't experienced it ourselves. Prepandemic, I saw it in an old friend when we met for cocktails at a popular happy hour spot in Washington, DC. The place was bustling with young, energetic professionals excitedly talking over drinks. You could feel the energy of their new careers; they were just beginning to feel the thrill of professional success.

My friend's dull expression was a stark contrast to this energy. She was going through a tough time at work and feeling disillusioned about her career. "I feel like I'm drifting," she said, "like I don't even know how or why I ended up here. I'm feeling so lost."

Many of us can relate to this feeling. At some time or another, you've probably been in a job that was unsatisfying and felt the heaviness of the daily grind. The sight of passionate, joyful, excited people irritated you. You'd remind yourself that not everyone can live their passion and joy; some people just need to pay the bills.

When I asked my friend what she was passionate about, she drew a blank. She said, "I used to love ceramics, but I don't have time for passion now. I'm too busy at work, and when I get home, I'm too exhausted to think about it. I'm just on this treadmill, and I can't stand it anymore."

This feeling of being lost and disconnected from passion and joy is widespread among adults. So many of us walk through life, feeling numb and desperate to be connected to our work, but we aren't sure how to get there. We buy self-help books and listen to podcasts and visit life coaches and psychologists, on a mission to find our passion and purpose, and a way to rekindle joy.

Can this be traced back to a joyless learning experience in school? Willis tells us: "The truth is that when we scrub joy and comfort from the classroom, we distance our students from effective information processing and long-term memory storage. Instead of taking pleasure from learning, students become bored, anxious, and anything but engaged. They ultimately learn to feel bad about school and lose the joy they once felt."[68]

If this sounds like your child, do not despair. Willis offers encouragement from her own experience as a neurologist and classroom teacher:[69]

Neuroimaging studies and measurement of brain chemical transmitters reveal that students' comfort level can influence information transmission and storage in the brain ... When students are engaged and motivated and feel minimal stress, information flows freely through the affective filter in the amygdala and they achieve higher levels of cognition, make connections, and experience 'aha' moments. Such learning comes not from quiet classrooms and directed lectures, but from classrooms with an atmosphere of exuberant discovery.

ADDING JOY TO DISTANCE LEARNING

Even if your child's school experience seems joyless, you can take simple steps to help foster an environment that will start rekindling that joy. Here are a few ways to start:

1. **Help your child advocate for more engaging learning.** To start, read the Zoom Boosters in Appendix VI and share them with your children's teachers, encouraging them to build more engagement into the school day. At home, you can also interact more with your children as they work by asking questions, inviting conversation, and getting curious about their assignments.

2. **Make it relevant.** Help your child connect the dots between what they are learning in school and their own lives. Teachers do not have time to make lessons personally interesting and motivating for every child. Help your child find their own answer for "Why are we learning about this?"

3. **Lower stress.** When stress in school is high, encourage your child to take a short break. They could eat lunch outside, do five minutes of stretching, or do a guided meditation on YouTube. Remind them to vary their position and posture throughout the day. These things, even though they are small, help to reduce stress.

4. **Make sure your child moves.** Engaging in physical activity is good for mental, psychological, and physical health. Encourage

your child to go for a walk, play outside, or even jump rope in place—anything to get their blood pumping for a few minutes and reset their brain.

5. **Make it fun and motivating.** Try to make distance learning more lighthearted by making jokes, playing music, or leaving notes on your child's desk. Tell them you are proud of them, and remind them how much they have had to unlearn and relearn. Celebrate the small stuff.

CONNECTING TO JOY

When someone is connected to their passion and joy, it is palpable. The person I know who embodies passion more than anyone else I've ever met is my brother.

While I was interested in telling stories and making movies, my brother had an early passion for space exploration. He was deeply moved by the Colorado sky at night, and he dreamed of traveling to the stars. Countless hours of *Star Wars* fueled his imagination and drove his dream to become an aerospace engineer or an astronaut. He became a math whiz and jumped three years ahead in his math classes at school. By fifth grade he was writing computer programs on early Apple computers, and by freshman year, he had taken all the math classes our high school offered. He planned to attend the Air Force Academy on his path to becoming an astronaut.

This dream was dashed when he was diagnosed with myopia. But he didn't let that stop him from following his passion. He graduated from the University of Virginia with a degree in aerospace engineering, went on to an internship with NASA, and finally landed a job writing software for a company that did spacecraft modeling.

A few years later, in 1998, he started the world's first space tourism company. Over the next decade he enabled the private missions of self-funded space explorers, including Dennis Tito, Anousheh Ansari, Richard Garriott, Guy Laliberté, and Charles Simonyi.

If my brother hadn't single-mindedly followed his passion, he may have let myopia crush his dreams forever. But the joy that space brought him—the same joy he felt as a kid watching *Star Wars* and gazing at the night sky—led him to overcome every obstacle and become a leading entrepreneur in the space industry. Today, his vision is to open space to all private citizens, and to procure and develop space-based resources for the benefit of humanity. And if you ever met him, you would feel his pure passion.

Whether your child decides to follow their passion by making cardboard rocket ships, joining a virtual band, learning to play tennis, or building robots, encourage them to embrace their joy.

This reminds me of a family in my local community. The boy, a sixth grader when the pandemic hit, knew that frontline workers needed masks. He also knew his mom was good at sewing. He let the joy of service lead him to set up shop in his mom's sewing room. He traced a mask pattern on yards of fabric, cutting out hundreds of masks for his mom to sew. The masks were picked up at their home by police officers and distributed to frontline workers. A month later, this mother and son team had made over one thousand masks, receiving lots of positive feedback for the masks with the Washington Capitals' logo, our local hockey team. The management of the Washington Capitals learned about this amazing duo, and their story was captured on video and played on television during the NHL playoffs. Did this young boy begin with a desire to be recognized on television? Of course not. He began with joy.

I have noticed (and I imagine you have too) that people who bind themselves to what brings them joy tend to thrive in some way, shape, or form—no matter what adversity they face. Have you ever seen a fragile sprout break through solid concrete? It's a marvel to see the tiny green stem reach toward the sun with such persistence and strength that it pushes through a road. Whether it be a crack in the road, or a crack in the school system, we can push through and keep reaching for the sun. As Joseph Campbell said, "We cannot cure the world of sorrows, but we can choose to live in joy."

As we've journeyed through the Seven Wonders, remember all that we have unlearned as a result of being forced into a totally new kind of schooling. Embrace the free time, and use it to be curious, to make things, to have hands-on experiences. Get outside, breathe the fresh air, ignite your creativity and your individuality, and find your place of joy.

Get outside, breathe the fresh air, ignite your creativity and your individuality, and find your place of joy.

This joy of learning will give your children fuel for life to power whatever path they choose. We just need to keep that joy alive. The good news is that it is entirely possible—as I found with my own children after our homeschool year.

A NEW RELATIONSHIP WITH SCHOOL

After our homeschool year, my children had a completely different relationship with school. They no longer viewed school as boring, unimaginative, and uninspiring. They no longer felt powerless in their learning. They gained an intrinsic desire to follow their curiosities, be creative, and explore their world.

When it came time to return to traditional school, we discovered that something wondrous happened. You know that feeling when you revisit a place from your childhood and it just looks so small? They had this experience with the concept of school.

After living outside the system for fifteen months, they gained the ability to see its walls. My children, young as they were, quickly came to understand that school is a system of learning, and not learning itself. Throughout the homeschool year, they began to articulate the strengths and weaknesses of schooling as a system because they actually had something to compare it to.

We spent a lot of time talking about schooling versus learning. Living outside the system, they could see the difference and imagine a better way. Many of the ideas in this book came from their experiences. Slowly, they began to fall in love with learning again. Curiosity bloomed. They discovered new passions, and learning became fun.

We didn't talk about grades or test scores. We shed labels. We removed limits. We reset expectations. We learned for the joy of learning, and that was enough. We learned fast and slow, took breaks and field trips, detours and diversions. We did a lot of learning outside. By stepping off the conveyer belt, my children found that their curiosity and learning could go in all directions, not just one. We developed a transformative new mindset that shattered the mental model we all held about school.

When our homeschooling year ended, the boys never viewed school in the same way. They were changed. There would be mornings when my children were tired or out of sorts, when they had a late sports practice or didn't finish an assignment, and I would say, "Sleep in; you can skip school today."

"I *want* to go to school today!" they would respond. To see this change in them was amazing. Children, no matter the age, *want* to feel engaged in learning. It doesn't matter if it's inside or outside school—they *want* to feel like what they do at school matters; the same way you and I want to feel like what we do at work matters. We know children feel the best about school when they think to themselves, *what I am learning is doing me good and will actually make a difference in my life.* We also know that this feeling doesn't come from external circumstances, but from *inside* the child.

For my children, the paradigm was completely flipped. They no longer wanted to get out of school; they wanted to get *into* learning. In many ways, they continued to redefine the school experience for themselves, even as their schools moved online in the spring of 2020, and they continue in a hybrid model for the foreseeable future.

All our children can use the Wonders in this book to help them face the challenges of the disruption of school with open minds, pro-actively exploring how to learn best in this changing world.

LEARNING DOESN'T BELONG TO SCHOOL; IT COMES FROM WITHIN

When you break free from the system and from its constraints, you can approach school with a completely different attitude, mindset, and frame of reference for what learning can be. Freed from the mentality that grades and tests are the be-all and end-all of learning, children can truly understand that learning is not external; learning is *internal.* That is the ultimate joy in this journey of Wonders: the realization that learning cannot be contained in a building or a classroom or a curriculum or a school system. Learning is contained *inside.*

The engine driving the joy of learning is not an external force. It comes from within. When you give your child the gift of the joy of learning, it allows them to say, "Learning is mine, and no one can take it away."

When your child owns their learning, it doesn't matter what

educational situation they find themselves in—whether it's a bad teacher or a boring curriculum or a lack of resources or even going to school over Zoom in the middle of the pandemic. They can carry that joy with them everywhere they go, from structured classes to impromptu learning opportunities. And they can carry that joy through a pandemic and right back into the structure of the educational system.

But what makes the joy of learning especially wondrous is that it doesn't stop when your child finishes school. A true joy of learning will stay with them for the rest of their lives.

THE JOY OF LEARNING IS LIFELONG

Embracing the Seven Wonders of Learning is not just about getting your child through school, or getting your child into college, or getting your child a good job. It's about giving them a gift that will last them the rest of their lives. Whatever they do once they graduate high school—whether they go to college or not, whether they go to graduate school or not—their love of learning will carry on. No matter their academic path, they'll continue to learn for their whole lives.

It doesn't matter whether your child knows early on what their passion is, or whether they are wandering around joyfully learning many different things. If they have the freedom to follow wherever their heart leads, that in and of itself will lead to a joy of learning. Just as a young adult living on their own for the first time feels elation when they realize they don't need permission to eat ice cream, a child will feel elation when they realize they don't need permission to learn about what interests them—they can just do it. That elation is what makes a lifelong learner.

Here is the marvelous bonus of this journey through the Wonders:

it may make a lifelong learner not only of your children, but of you as well. You may find your own joy of learning rekindled. That is certainly what happened to me during our homeschool year.

You might be surprised to learn that after the homeschool sabbatical, my husband and I both prioritized going back to school. He chose to study business leadership at the Jack Welch Management Institute, and I enrolled in an exciting program at Drexel University, one of a few universities in the world offering a master of science degree in creativity and innovation.

Why would we step outside the system only to step back in? Because, as a family, we fell in love with learning. My husband and I wanted to set an example of self-driven curiosity and lifelong learning for our children, inside or outside of school. We wanted to model that with this new mindset, school could be different and better than before.

JOY OF LEARNING, JOY IN LIFE

As I conclude the writing of this book, the pandemic is still a global health crisis that is disrupting our lives in immeasurable ways. Still, we are finding joy. How? Because humans are incredibly resilient, and joy—true joy—is unshakable. While happiness is based on external circumstances and is often the first thing to fall when faced with adversity, joy comes from within. Once it is kindled, it can survive even the darkest night. In fact, it is in the dark of night that we can see just how brightly joy shines.

It is in the dark of night that we can see just how brightly joy shines.

Out of curiosity, I Googled "pandemic rediscovering joy"—and was awestruck by the results. There was story after story, blog post after blog post, article after article about people rediscovering their joy in cooking, being in nature, playing an instrument, painting, riding a bike, reading—and even rediscovering the joy in relationships and marriages that had been buried under the hecticness of regular day-to-day life.

The rediscovery of the joy of learning is our final Wonder, but the light of that joy can radiate out into all areas of your children's lives—and into your own.

PASSING THE TORCH

With this final Wonder, you are giving your child their own torch to carry into the future. By rekindling their joy of learning, you are giving them the light by which they will find their way through school, through the world, and through their lives. By the light of this torch, I hope they will be able to follow the stirrings of their hearts, find their passions, and live a life full of learning and joy for the rest of their days.

KEY TAKEAWAYS

- When children learn in a joyless environment, over time their brains learn to disengage, impacting attention and memory.

- Following the stirrings of your heart leads to joy of learning.

- Binding yourself to your passions radiates joy and leads to success.

- If you rekindle a joy of learning in your child, it will carry over when they reenter the educational system.

- Learning comes from within.

- The joy of learning is a lifelong gift.

WHAT NEXT? FIVE WAYS TO BRING
THIS CHAPTER TO LIFE

- **Think:** Think about someone you know who possesses a joy of learning. Reflect on this person's attributes and where that joy might come from.

- **Feel:** When have you felt the joy of learning? Why? When have you not felt the joy of learning? Why? Notice the difference between these two feelings.

- **Do:** Ask your children to take note every day of one thing (or more!) that brings them joy. And while you're at it, do this yourself as well. Share your moments of joy over dinner, at breakfast the next day—or whenever you feel like it!

- **Act:** Embrace lifelong learning by considering what you want to learn more about—and do it. Share your learning with your children. Ask your child's teachers where joy shows up in their classrooms and reflect on what they say.

- **Discuss:** Discuss with your children how prepandemic school made them feel about learning. How do they feel now, in the midst of the pandemic? Continue having this discussion periodically as you make the shifts in thinking and practice what we've discussed in this book.

PERSONAL CHECK-IN: WHAT ARE YOU THINKING?

- How could I embrace more joy in my life?

- What could I start learning that would bring me joy?

- How might I nurture more joy in my child's learning?

- How will I bring the Seven Wonders of Learning into my family?

A NEW BEGINNING

*Change will not come if we wait for some other person,
or if we wait for some other time. We are the ones we've
been waiting for. We are the change that we seek.*

—BARACK OBAMA

At this moment, we are at a crossroads. We left the status quo and experienced the pain and fear of the disruption. We felt the bottom drop out from under us and wondered how to navigate the chaos and uncertainty. Over the course of this book and our journey through the Seven Wonders, I hope you have started to find your way to a transformational turning point, from which we can find the possibility of building a new and better normal.

We have the opportunity to shift the paradigm of what education is, to rekindle our children's joy of learning, and to light the torch for them to carry through the rest of their lives. But we have to make the active choice to keep that torch burning. We have to make the choice to not let it be snuffed out again by the structure of the education system. We've reached the moment where we need to make the choice to change the status quo.

This pandemic is unlike anything we have experienced. We have all suffered—and we have learned so much. We now have the opportunity to make a lasting difference in the way our children learn. What a waste it would be to settle back into our old ways of thinking about school.

The truth is, we've come too far to turn back now. Our children have experienced learning outside of the school building. They are as far away from the Seneca Schoolhouse as they've ever been. They have seen the educational system broken in a way no other living generation has experienced. And they will be the ones who continue to break the system and improve it for the better—if we encourage them.

Let's use the momentum of this large-scale disruption to accelerate positive change. As parents, let's dare to carry this new mindset forward and co-create a better way. Let's resist the urge to slide back into the prepandemic status quo.

Most importantly, let's encourage our children to be agents of change who speak up, speak out, and self-advocate for their own learning. And when they dead-end against century-old thinking, which they will, let's help them see it for what it is—antiquated. Let's embolden them to use their innate curiosity and creativity to change school forever.

Right now, we don't know what's on the other side of this pandemic. The challenges we are facing—as a society and as individual families—are real and serious. But, as I said in the introduction, I believe we will look back at 2020 and realize that it triggered positive growth, adaptation, and innovation.

This disruption is a new beginning—for parents, teachers, our children, and our children's children—to light the way for a better way to learn.

APPENDICES

APPENDIX I: HOMESCHOOLING RESOURCES

Here are some of my favorite homeschooling resources:

- Art for Kids Hub Guided Drawing
  (**www.artforkidshub.com**)

- ABCya (**www.abcya.com**)

- Bill Nye the Science Guy (**www.billnye.com**)

- Bottle Biology (**www.bottlebiology.org**)

- BrainPOP (**www.brainpop.com**)

- Daily Grammar (**www.dailygrammar.com**)

- DreamBox Learning (**www.dreambox.com**)

- Edmund Scientifics Online (**www.scientificsonline.com**)

- Enchanted Learning (**www.enchantedlearning.com**)

- Envision Mathematics
  (**www.savvas.com/index.cfm?locator=PS37Dc**)

- Everyday Spelling (**www.everydayspelling.com**)

- HowStuffWorks "Science Channel"
  (**www.science.howstuffworks.com**)

- IXL (**www.ixl.com**)

- Johns Hopkins Center for Talented Youth (www.cty.jhu.edu)

- K12 (www.k12.com)

- Khan Academy (www.khanacademy.org)

- KinderArt (www.kinderart.com)

- Lakeshore Learning (www.lakeshorelearning.com)

- Musicnotes (www.musicnotes.com)

- Outschool (www.outschool.com)

- Popular Mechanics for Kids
  (available on Amazon or YouTube)

- Reading A-Z (www.readinga-z.com)

- Scratch (www.scratch.mit.edu)

- TED Talks (www.ted.com)

- The Great Courses (www.thegreatcourses.com)

- The Magic School Bus (www.kids.scholastic.com/kids/books/the-magic-school-bus/)

- The Young Scientists Club (www.theyoungscientistsclub.com)

- Time4Learning (www.time4learning.com)

- Young Rembrandts (www.YoungRembrandts.com)

APPENDIX II: SIXTY-FIVE BOREDOM BUSTERS

When your kids are bored, help them brainstorm possible activities, but make it clear that it's their job to figure out how to enjoy their own time. This whopping list should help get their creative juices flowing!

The List of Awesome Ideas

1. Make a book (a fiction story, a nonfiction story, a coloring book, a joke book—anything!).

2. Build a fort with blankets and pillows—and whatever else you can find.

3. Write someone a letter (Grandpa, Nona, Bubbie, the president, a favorite teacher, people in the hospital, anyone!).

4. Go to a park, or go to a variety of parks and compare them. Take pictures from the top of every slide. Master every set of monkey bars. Swing on every swing.

5. Take on the One Hundreds Challenge. Do one hundred squats, one hundred push-ups, and one hundred sit-ups every day for thirty days. Or pick different exercises like one hundred jumping jacks, burpees, or lunges. For fun, time how long it takes to do the challenge every day, and chart your improvement over time.

6. Put on some music and dance it out. Have someone occasionally stop the music to freeze dance. Or sign up to learn specific dance moves on **www.steezy.co**, **www.udemy.com**, or **www.outschool.com**.

7. Decorate the mirror or the shower wall with lipstick, finger paint, or shaving cream. Trace your face in a silly self-portrait, practice the alphabet, or make designs. Then wash the mirror with a sponge.

8. Write down ten things you love about each person in your family. Give each person the list with a big hug. Now write down ten things you love about yourself, and post the list next to your bed.

9. Go outside and lie down in a safe place. Bring a friend or a pet. Find shapes in the clouds. Find birds in the trees. Imagine what's way up there past the sky. Soak up some vitamin D.

10. Wash your favorite toys (or the dishes!). Fill the bathtub with tons of soapy water and have fun scrubbing any of your submersible toys. Wash anything else that needs it—like your yoga mat!

11. See how many times you can dribble the basketball (or soccer ball). Keep trying again and again until you get to one hundred, and then set a higher goal. Now, try a Hula-Hoop, juggling, or something new.

12. Paint, draw, or trace a picture from your imagination. Or try a guided drawing on **www.artforkidshub.com, www.youngrembrandts.com**, or **www.outschool.com**. For fun, take a time-lapse video of your drawing coming to life.

13. Wash the car. Even better, enlist the help of your siblings to wash the car with you, and have a hose or soapsuds battle. Add water balloons to the fun. Now wash the cobwebs off your bike.

14. Plan a treasure hunt with clues. Ask a parent, sibling, or friend to write the clues and make them tricky to solve. Or organize an online or Zoom treasure or scavenger hunt with friends you cannot see in person.

15. Ride your bike. Safely try riding your bike in new ways, such as with your feet sticking out sideways, or with one hand (or no hands) on the handlebars. Decorate your bicycle helmet or your bike. Try adding accessories to your bike, like a horn, a reflector,

or lights, or noisemakers for the spokes. Learn to inflate your bike tires or replace the chain when it falls off.

16. Make a scene in a cardboard box, or turn a cardboard box into something creative! Take several discarded Amazon boxes and interconnect them to make a giant cardboard box sculpture. Look up "cardboard box sculptures" on Google Images for ultimate inspiration.

17. Start a journal of any kind, or write in a journal you already started. Use different-colored pens to make it fun. Cut out inspiring pictures or quotes, and tape or glue them into the journal pages. Try sketching household objects, things from nature, or wacky inventions in your journal. Who cares if it looks sloppy; just be creative! Search "da Vinci's notebooks" on Google just for fun to learn about how da Vinci wrote from right to left and drew all kinds of wacky inventions.

18. Make homemade wrapping paper. Using materials you can find around your house, in nature, or in your trash or recycle bin, make some unique wrapping paper. Search "DIY wrapping paper" for tons of cool ideas.

19. Organize your room—your way! Whether it's color-coding your closet, sorting LEGOs, arranging stuffed animals on your headboard, or displaying trophies and medals in a new way, have fun making your space just the way you like it. Bonus: Make signs telling siblings to keep out!

20. Make a concoction in the kitchen. Ask a parent if you can use random ingredients to mix up a batch of creative stew, or use vinegar and baking soda to make a big fizz! When your concoction is done, freeze it and check on it a few hours later. Dare someone to eat it!

21. Create a cool sculpture out of trash or junk. Don't let those toilet paper rolls and egg cartons go to waste! Gather a pile of junk, and transform it into something spectacular. Create your own recycled art gallery, and charge your family members admission to marvel at your creations!

22. Create a play, or make a movie with real costumes. Think of what you like best about your favorite movies like *Star Wars, Harry Potter, The Avengers,* or *Frozen.* Now invent your own characters, make costumes from things you already have, and make a movie using a phone or video camera. Don't forget to play with slow motion just for fun!

23. Use pictures from magazines, newspapers, or printed images from the internet to make a collage. Add layers of your own style until it's just right, and then give your artwork a name. Don't forget to sign it!

24. Create a circus performance. Create your own three-ring (or however-many-rings!) circus at home. Use Hula-Hoops, tennis balls, balloons, pets, siblings, bikes, scooters, and whatever else you can find that your imaginary audiences will love to watch.

25. Make your room (or any room in the house) into a rain forest. Put up pictures of plants, trees, and animals. Play jungle sound effects. Eat bananas.

26. Make an obstacle course. Use cardboard boxes, furniture, toys, or whatever you can find; then challenge a sibling or parent to see who can get through it the fastest.

27. Invent a secret language. Write it down in a notebook. Share it with a sibling or friend, and memorize it so you can have whole conversations without anyone else understanding.

28. Make up a secret code with a decoder. Get ideas from these codes: **www.learnincolor.com/secret-spy-codes-for-kids.html**. Learn them with a friend or a sibling, and leave coded messages for each other around the house or neighborhood. For extra fun, make a decoder ring, use invisible ink, or use a flashlight to learn Morse code.

29. Read a book, or try reading two books at the same time! Read two books by the same author, or two books on the same subject, or two books in which the main character has the same name. How do they compare?

30. Have a water balloon fight (outside!). Create a name and a mascot for your side in the water balloon battle. Write a fight song for your side. Create a bunker to hide in, or camouflage armor to sneak up on the enemy side. Try making a water balloon piñata and smashing it with pool noodles.

31. Memorize a poem and recite it for your parents. Or write your own poem, memorize it, and recite it for your parents! Add a costume and a wig and record your poem on video. Visit **www.poetry.org** to find poems. This site also has links to lots of other poetry sites!

32. Come up with business ideas and write them down. If you had a business, what would it do or make? What would the name of the business be? Design logos for your different businesses.

33. Make a boat using a plastic soda bottle base and Popsicle sticks. Then make more boats out of different materials, such as cardboard, duct tape, tin cans, and bottles (the recycling bin is a great place to look for materials!). Then float your boats in a pond or stream or the bathtub, and see which floats best.

34. Draw a picture of a desert island with all the things you would want on it. What food would you want? What favorite books and music? What pets? Which friends and family members would you want with you? Which celebrities or fictional characters would you want to be stranded with?

35. Blindfold your sibling and take them on a tour of your house and yard. Have them guess where they are by using their five senses, including listening, smelling, and touching objects, or by offering them clues about what's in the room or environment. Then switch places and have them do it for you!

36. Play a board game. If you don't have any in your house that you want to play, there are many games available online on sites like en.boardgamearena.com, www.tabletopia.com, and www.boardgamesonline.net.

37. Create your own board game. Try making one based off your favorite book or movie. Download templates from www.boardgamesmaker.com or www.thegamecrafter.com, or make your own out of paper, cardboard, and markers or colored pencils. Find little objects around the house or outside to serve as pieces for the players.

38. See if you can draw a picture with your foot. See if you can draw with your nondominant hand. See if you can draw with your eyes closed. See if you can draw with your foot with your eyes closed! See if you can draw with your teeth. Enlist your siblings. Draw each other in crazy ways!

39. Draw on the sidewalk with chalk. See how big of a drawing you can create. Can you create a drawing that stretches the entire

block? Watch a tutorial online about how to draw a sidewalk mural and be inspired!

40. Play hopscotch. How long of a hopscotch board can you make and successfully complete? Try variations of the game, like the ones described here: **www.parents.com/fun/activities/hopscotch**, or create your own variations!

41. Play jump rope. Jump to the rhythm of your favorite song. Make up a funny rhyming poem to jump rope to. See how many times you can jump without tripping. Can you make it to one hundred? Two hundred? Find a friend to try double Dutch. Try to shuffle dance while jump roping. Have fun!

42. Play with bubbles in the sink. Add soap to water and see how big a bubble you can form. Try to get one bubble to stack on top of another. Add food coloring. Get a piece of paper and colored pencils and see if you can capture the iridescent colors of the bubbles.

43. Make a garden. You can do this in the backyard, or you can make a window box garden. What kinds of plants do you want to grow? Vegetables? Flowers? Herbs?

44. Make puppets with old socks, buttons, and markers. Recreate your favorite stories based on the plot of your favorite book, movie, or television show. Write your own play, and perform it with the sock puppets.

45. Make a list of fun things you can do without talking. Invent some new games that are totally silent. Try playing them in the car, when your parents are on a conference call, or when your siblings are taking tests.

46. Mix liquid hand soap, cornstarch, and food coloring into paint and paint the bathtub. Try painting a different picture on every tile. Try painting a series of pictures in the tiles that make a story, like panels in a comic book.

47. Make lemonade, or cookies, or Rice Krispies treats and set up a stand to sell them. Don't forget the hand sanitizer!

48. Read the dictionary and find as many *weird* words as possible. What words look like they are totally made up? What words sound really funny when you say them out loud? Make a list of these words. Try to put them all into a short story or poem.

49. Build five different kinds of paper airplanes, and see which one flies best. Find patterns on **www.foldnfly.com**; then make up some of your own. Measure how far they each fly. Try launching them from different places—standing on the ground or from off the porch or out of a window.

50. Challenge yourself to write a story that is *exactly* one hundred words long. If it's over or under one hundred words, edit it until it is exactly one hundred. Try writing a one-hundred-word story in which most of the words start with the same letter. Use a thesaurus to find synonyms for words that start with that letter!

51. Build a long domino run. How many dominoes can you successfully create a run with if they're in a straight line? How about if there are lots of curves? Create a domino run that is a picture of something.

52. Camp out inside. Set up a tent in the living room or make a tent out of blankets and chairs. Turn off all the lights and use a flashlight. Tell scary stories!

53. Learn a new magic trick. Start with the ones here: **www.care.com/c/stories/4051/easy-magic-tricks-for-kids/**. Use Google, YouTube, or Instagram to find more once you've mastered those. Then try inventing your own magic trick!

54. Learn a new survival skill and practice it. Learn how to tie different kinds of knots for different purposes (start here: **www.animatedknots.com/basic-knots**). Learn how to read a compass, and practice using it to navigate around your neighborhood.

55. Take a walk, but don't ever look at the ground (it's hard!). See how far you can get without stumbling! Can you make it all the way around the block?

56. Go to the library, or Audible, Apple Books, or the Kindle Store, and find three books on *totally new* subjects. What's something you have never read a book about? Ask a librarian or parent for help if you aren't sure where to start, or if you can't find a book on the subject you're interested in.

57. Pretend you are a spy, and get new information. Keep a notebook with you, and make notes about the goings-on in your neighborhood. Did a neighbor get a new haircut? Did the house next door get new curtains? What is the name of the dog that lives at the end of the street?

58. Create a comic book hero, and make a graphic novel. What is the hero's name? What are their superpowers? What does their costume look like? Who is their archnemesis? Do they have a sidekick?

59. Pick a favorite song, and try to sing it in multiple styles. Can you sing it like a rapper, opera singer, country singer, or jazz singer?

Perform the different styles for your family. Now try writing your own song and performing it live or recording it on video or audio.

60. Read a book on video and then watch yourself. Play around with different voices for different characters. Dress up in different clothes. Watch it, and then try it again with totally different clothes and voices!

61. Take apart an old electronic to see how it works. Then see if you can put it back together again and get it working!

62. Conduct an experiment about anything! Think of a hypothesis and test it. Conduct the experiment multiple times, writing down the results each time. Ask "What happens if … " and see where it leads!

63. Look at something under a microscope. It can be something from outside—a leaf, a dead bug, a bit of dirt. It can be something from inside—a thread, a drop of dish soap, a crumb of bread. Try to draw what you see.

64. Make a short book to teach Mom or Dad something you learned at school. Don't forget to include illustrations! Try writing a book that rhymes!

65. Write down ten inventions that would make your life better, easier, or more fun! Pick a couple to design. Draw out how you think they would work. Then, see if you can build a prototype out of cardboard, string, duct tape, et cetera!

Now, add your own!

APPENDIX III: SEVENTY-FIVE OPEN-ENDED QUESTIONS

Open-ended questions are those that have no definitive right or wrong answers. They lead to conversation and maybe even more questions. Here are some ideas, many with fill in the blanks to help you apply these questions in all types of situations.

1. Between _____ and _____, which do you like better and why?

2. Can you explain more about _____ to me? Tell me more.

3. Compare _____ and _____. How are they different? How are they similar?

4. Describe what the future of _____ looks like in your imagination.

5. Does anything about _____ surprise you? Why or why not?

6. Give _____ a rating of one to five. Why did you choose that number?

7. How can I help you with _____? Tell me three ways.

8. How could you turn your biggest weakness into your greatest strength? Explain.

9. How do you define success as it relates to _____? Tell me more.

10. How does learning about _____ relate to everyday life? Think of three ways.

11. How is your current situation of _____ like something you have experienced before?

12. How many solutions can you think of to the problem of _____? Name at least three solutions.

13. How would you change _____ if you could? Why?

14. If you could change anything about _____, assuming no limits to your imagination, what would it be and why?

15. If you could do one thing to improve your situation with _____, what would it be and why?

16. If you could go back and change one thing about _____, what would it be and why?

17. If you could go on an adventure with anyone to anywhere, where would it be and with who? Why?

18. If you could have any job in the world, what would it be and why?

19. If you could make anything, what would it be? What materials would you need to get started?

20. If you could travel _____ years back in time to visit your younger self, what advice would you give yourself and why? If you could travel _____ years forward in time and visit your future self, what advice would you give yourself and why?

21. If you get really curious about _____, what does it make you think, question, and wonder?

22. If you had a magic power, which one would it be and why?

23. If you were a teacher, what would you teach your students and why?

24. In facing this challenge of _____, how have you solved similar challenges before?

25. In which areas of your life do you feel strongest/weakest/most in need of help? Why?

26. Name five things that are important to you in life right now that were not important before. Why are they important now?

27. Of all the things you are learning right now, what will be the most useful when you are an adult?

28. Tell me how you had the idea for _____. What was your inspiration? What comes next?

29. Tell me three details about _____?

30. Think about _____ problem in your life. Come up with at least twenty questions about the problem. Which is most helpful in solving the problem and why?

31. Think of an important person, including you. What are the five best traits of this person? Why?

32. Think of something you made or want to make. How would you know if it was just good or if it was excellent?

33. What are some of the best/worst decisions you've made related to _____?

34. What are three differences between _____ and _____? Which stands out most?

35. What are you looking most forward to this week, this month, this year?

36. What are you most excited about right now? In school? In life? With your friends?

37. What are you most thankful for as it relates to _____?

38. What caused you to behave the way you did when you did _____?

39. What characteristics make a person a good friend? Why?

40. What did you expect to learn/do/think/feel in _____situation, compared with what you actually learned/did/thought/felt in that situation?

41. What do you consider to be your top five talents? Think of ten ways you can use these talents today.

42. What do you know how to do that you could teach others? Who would you teach and why?

43. What do you love doing more than anything else? What is stopping you from doing it more?

44. What do you miss most from prepandemic life and school? Why? What do you miss the least? Why?

45. What do you think about when you first wake up? What about when you are falling asleep?

46. What do you think caused this situation you are experiencing? What do you think will happen next?

47. What five words best describe you? What five words would _____use to describe you? Why do you think these words are the same or different?

48. What if there were no limits on your imagination, what would you do next? Why?

49. What is one area in your life you wish you had more control over? Why?

50. What is something that you really want to do, but need a new skill to do it? What's next?

51. What is something that you want, but do not have the courage to ask for? What are you afraid of?

52. What is something you always wanted to tell me? How do you imagine I will react if you tell me?

53. What is the best advice you have ever received from _____? Why?

54. What is the most fun things about _____?

55. What is the most wonderful/worst thing about _____? How might these things change?

56. What is your biggest dream? Can you visualize it? What does it look like? Share three details.

57. What is your favorite family tradition? Why? How could you make it even better?

58. What is your motivation for doing _____? What does this motivation feel like? Where does it come from?

59. What is your motto? Explain why it is significant to you.

60. What kind of feedback can you give me on _____? What would you like feedback on?

61. What makes someone creative? What is the difference between creative and artistic?

62. What makes someone smart? What is the difference between smart and wise?

63. What makes you laugh the most, and why? Who always makes you laugh?

64. What new activities would like you like try? Tell me why these things are interesting to you?

65. What one question would you ask your biggest role model and why?

66. What are the top priorities for you today, this week, this month, this year?

67. What were you thinking when you said/did _____?

68. What were you trying to accomplish when you did _____? Describe the outcome.

69. What would you try if you knew you would not fail? What stops you from going for it?

70. What's your favorite and least favorite _____ and why?

71. When do you feel stressed? When you feel this way, what makes you feel better?

72. When do you most daydream? What do you daydream about?

73. Which of your accomplishments are you most proud of today, this week, this month, this year?

74. Who are your three best role models, and why?

75. Who or what influences your life the most? Tell me more.

APPENDIX IV: BUILDING A "BACK ROOM" MAKER SPACE

As we talked about in chapter 4, every child needs a space to build, make, and do things with their hands. Creating this space does not need to cost a lot of money, take a lot of time, or even look that great. It does not even need to be an entire room; in most cases a small alcove, closet, or a rolling cart or folding table will do the trick. I've developed a simple acronym to guide parents through the process of creating a hands-on space for their child, and it's super easy to remember: I MAKE.

I Is for *Individualized*

Before you get started, spend some time thinking about your specific child. What is their individual interest in building, making, or doing? What will he or she make in this space? Will your child take apart computers, paint canvases, try recipes, use clay to sculpt, design topiaries, perform piano music, record podcasts, program video games, record workout videos, repair bikes, make ultimate trick shots with basketballs, design custom sneakers, make horror films, build furniture, animate in virtual reality, make exploding concoctions, test new business ideas, launch model rockets, or do makeup tutorials? There are so many unique ways that kids can get hands-on with their passions and interests, so start by being clear about your child's individualized goals for their space.

M Is for *Materials* and Tools

Next, ask yourself what basic materials and tools will support your child's goals. Do you need to provide paint and brushes, lumber and power tools, wires and circuits, fabric remnants, yardsticks, and a sewing kit, or potting soil and garden tools? What about safety goggles, gloves, and other protective gear to keep your child safe?

Start with a small supply of the basic materials your child will need to build or make. You can most likely find starter materials in your own home, at garage sales, or at discount stores. One of the best places to look is in your own recycle bin. You will be amazed at what kids can do with a few materials and tools as well as an accessible space that is all their own.

A Is for *Accessible* Space

Once you know what materials and tools your child will need, think carefully about how to make these supplies easily accessible for your child. For example, if your child wants to create art, what is the most accessible space for art supplies? This could mean putting supplies in a cardboard box, a drawer, or a shelf in a closet. If your child needs tools to disassemble old broken electronics, maybe you can allocate space in a corner of a garage, basement, or outside? If your child wants to grow a small garden, perhaps garden tools could be most accessible in a plastic bin stored outside? If your child is creating music, consider using a rolling cart for music books, headphones, and lyric journals that can be stored right by the piano or keyboard. Giving your child easy and autonomous accessibility to what they want to make in a readily available location is what will set your child up to be successful.

K Is for *Kingdom*

Once your child has some basic materials and an accessible space, they need to feel like it is their own little kingdom of creativity. Your child should feel free to try new things, make mistakes, make a mess, and experiment without other people peering over their shoulder to inspect and judge their work. As you are thinking about where this space should be, consider how to protect your child's kingdom. I have seen parents put up a little privacy curtain or choose rooms that are away from the main action of the household. I've seen small folding tables on patios, in closets, and in garages. I have seen a writer's cart that can be rolled anywhere and everywhere, depending on where the child's inspiration strikes. For this space to fulfill its purpose, your child's kingdom needs to be a place where making can happen over days and weeks and months, not neatly wiped down at the end of the day and forgotten.

E Is for *Encouragement*

Just because your child has a kingdom of creativity does not mean they will run there every day. Just like anything else, it takes encouragement. Help your child learn that getting hands-on in their special space will help them beat boredom, release stress, get creative, have fun, and be inspired. Make a snack and take it to them while they make stuff. If you come across new materials that they would like, leave them out for your child to discover in their space. Leave little motivation notes that show them that you notice and value what they are building, making, and doing. Do not ever criticize or critique; instead, comment and question. Be adaptable—as your child figures out what they want to explore, let them adjust their space to fit their needs. And let them adjust it again when what they want to make changes again. This is the iterative cycle; it's best to just embrace it!

With this handy-dandy approach, it's totally OK to keep it simple. Your child's space to build, make, and do does not need to live up to anyone else's standards. It does not need to look like a professional makerspace, HGTV art studio, woodworker's workshop, or Pixar animator's office. You don't need to start with expensive color-coded bins and elaborate materials, pegboard toolholders, or fancy 3-D printers and Arduino IDEs. Just start with baby steps and a place to actively support your child as they get hands-on with their passions.

Just go for it and have fun!

APPENDIX V: EIGHTY ZOOM BOOSTERS

Be part of the solution in making distance and hybrid learning more fun and engaging by sharing this Big List of Zoom Boosters with children and teachers. I hope this list will spark even more ideas to add more excitement and joy to online learning. Please note, while the ideas below reference Zoom, they could be adapted for other online learning platforms. Enjoy!

1. **Twenty Questions.** This classic game works great on Zoom. The teacher gives one child the answer via private message; then other students ask yes-or-no questions to deduce the answer. Students can use the chat or raise hand feature to offer guesses. Also works great as a "get to know you" game.

2. **Alphabet Game.** Pick any theme or topic, and then ask students to say a word that relates to that theme or topic starting with *A* and moving consecutively through each letter of the alphabet. To organize speaking order, the teacher can display names in a predefined list via screen share.

3. **Animal Show and Share.** As a special event, students are invited to show their pets or stuffed animals and share a few facts. At the end of the show and share, the teacher presents a poll via screenshare to help the students reflect on what they learned.

4. **Baby Picture Game.** The teacher asks students to submit baby or toddler pictures in advance. During class, the teacher puts up the pictures one at a time. Students try to match their classmates with the pictures via polling or chat.

5. **Bingo.** There are many ways to play bingo via Zoom. Try **www.bingobaker.com** for ready-made bingo boards, or customize your own. The teacher can screenshare an online bingo generator

like **www.appzaza.com/bingo-number-generator** to automate the bingo caller role. Students can also play virtual bingo using **www.myfreebingocards.com**.

6. **Blackout.** To make math engaging and interactive, try playing virtual Blackout. The teacher assigns Blackout boards to students. Then players take turns rolling two dice and coloring in corresponding squares on their boards. There are many online dice-rolling generators to make this easy for all players, like **www.calculator.net/dice-roller.html**. Usually, the first student to fully color in their board wins. Also works well with smaller groups of kids in breakout rooms.

7. **Caption or "Name It" Game.** The teacher finds a funny photo, comic, or video to show the class using screenshare. The teacher divides students into small breakouts and gives each group five minutes to come up with the best caption. Reinforce a G-rating, and then wait for the laughs. As an option, the teacher can share a poll and let the class vote on a winner.

8. **Charades.** This old standard translates easily to Zoom. Split the class into two teams, and use a charades idea generator like **www.getcharadesideas.com** to choose words or phrases. The person acting out the charade uses the Zoom "spotlight" feature, and their team has one minute to correctly guess via talking or chat. Then, the other team does the same.

9. **Collaborative Brainstorming.** Teachers show students how to use any free online mind mapping software to visualize collaborative idea generation. Then the teacher breaks students into groups and sends them to breakouts to visually brainstorm ideas relevant to a topic or theme. Try **www.mindmeister.com** and **www.mindmup.com** among many free tools.

10. **Collaborative or Directed Drawing.** Use the whiteboard feature in Zoom or an application like **www.sketchboard.io** to draw a collaborative picture or communal art piece around a theme. For example, depict a scene from a book, a historical event, or a science experiment. Tools like Vibe and Jamboard give everyone art tools to help create a single image.

11. **Connect 4.** This classic game is easy to play virtually using **www.connect-4.org/en.** Teachers can motivate students to stay engaged with a short play break. For example, start the week with a bracket of players and continue on until just two finalists remain. Then, using screenshare, let all students watch the final matchup and cheer on the winners via chat.

12. **Crosswords and Word Searches.** Teachers can help kids engage with class content by making interactive crosswords and word searches. There are many available online tools including **www.en.crosswordsarena.com**, where an account is needed to play.

13. **Digitally Co-create.** Instead of a traditional written essay or test, teachers invite students to collaboratively work on creative projects in multimedia formats. Students can choose applications like Adobe Spark, Prezi, Google Slides, iMovie, or Podbeam and Anchor for podcasts. When first drafts are done, teachers ask students to submit projects for peer review and feedback. Then students revise, tweak, and iterate before submitting creative projects.

14. **Emoji Infographics.** Students take screenshots of their favorite emojis. Other categories could include least favorite emojis, emojis most misused by parents, and more. The teacher divides students into breakout groups and asks them to develop a creative

infographic revealing emoji trends among students in that group. Then the teacher invites all the students back together to share and compare results.

15. **Escape Rooms.** Teachers can create DIY Escape rooms using Google Forms, or divide students into breakouts to create their own DIY Escape Rooms. Before starting, the creator needs to pick the theme or story, identify how many lock questions and answers will be part of the journey, define questions and answers, and decide what happens upon escape. To work up to DIY, teachers can show students a variety of free online escape rooms like the Minecraft Escape Room, Harry Potter Escape Room, Space Exploration Escape Room, Escape the Fairy Tale, and many others that can be found online.

16. **Fact or Fiction**. To liven up the energy, teachers share a unique, strange, or unexpected fun fact about a topic or theme. Students vote to see if they think it is fact or fiction. If teachers solicit a fun fact about each student in advance, this is also a great way for kids to get know their peers online.

17. **Finish the Conversation Movie Clip Dialogue.** To add a burst of creativity to online class, a teacher shares a short scene of dialogue from a popular movie or cartoon. The teacher stops the clip short at an unexpected moment and asks the students to humorously finish the dialogue.

18. **First Letter Game.** The teacher puts up a letter via screenshare— for example, the letter E. Then the teacher names a category and asks students to come up with a word starting with the defined letter that matches the category. For added fun, try this random category generator: **www.capitalizemytitle.com/ random-topic-generator/**.

19. **Five Fingers.** All students put up one hand with fingers showing. The teacher names off a variety of life experiences like "knows how to make scrambled eggs" or "has been to the beach." Any player that has that life experience puts a finger down. The game goes on until the last person puts their last finger down. This activity can be adapted to ask questions about a thematic area of study.

20. **Five Things.** The teacher asks one student to name a topic and a classmate. That person has twenty seconds to name five items within that topic and then name another classmate. In turn, that person has twenty seconds to name five items within that topic and then another person. This can continue for as long as the class is enjoying the break.

21. **Flash Fiction.** The teacher divides students into breakouts and gives each group the same writing prompt for a sixty-second work of flash fiction. It could focus on a theme, location, character, or specific item that must be incorporated into a short dialogue. For example: Write a sixty-second drama that includes a spoon, the color green, a doorbell, a bird, and a cowboy boot. After a period of time in breakouts, the groups come back together and perform their sixty-second works of flash fiction, usually with much laughter.

22. **Get Moving.** The teacher creates an assignment that requires physical activity. For example, during lengthy stretches of distance learning, the teacher tells students to listen to a podcast while walking, or the teacher assigns small breakout groups to do facilitated movement like dance, yoga, tai chi, or sing-alongs like "Head, Shoulders, Knees, and Toes." The teacher should also ask older students to take turns leading these movement breaks.

23. **Google Translate Telephone Game.** The teacher selects a few students to facilitate the game. Each facilitator opens Google Translate. The teacher asks a question based on course content. The first student types the answer into Google Translate and selects a language for translation. The next student copies the translation and pastes it into Google Translate, selecting a new language for translation. Finally, the last facilitator translates the answer back into English. The whole class enjoys seeing if the answer is still correct.

24. **Guess What It Is.** Using screenshare, the teacher reveals just part of an image or object. It could be an extreme close-up or just one part of a bigger image. Using the chat or raise hand features, students guess what the image could be.

25. **Guess Who?** The teacher selects one student to be the guesser. The guesser picks a classmate and direct messages the teacher with the name. The rest of the class tries to guess who by narrowing down traits. For instance, a student might ask, "Does your person have glasses?" or "Does your person have dark hair?" When a correct guess is made, that student becomes the guesser.

26. **Haiku Writing.** A teacher writes a haiku about a well-known person. The teacher reads the haiku aloud, and students try to guess who the haiku describes. Then the teacher gives the students ten to fifteen minutes to write a haiku about themselves. The next day, the teacher reads the haikus aloud, and the students guess which classmate it describes. This is a great way for students to get to know each other.

27. **Hangman.** For a quick break, play hangman. There are many virtual versions of this game, including **www.hangmanwordgame. com**, which uses a robot image instead of a stick figure. Students

can play by themselves or challenge other students for some social interaction.

28. **Heads-Up**. This popular mobile app game is best played in Zoom breakout groups. One student holds the mobile app against their forehead while students try to describe the word to them so they can guess it. If students do not have the mobile app, they could make paper cards or use a random word generator via screen share.

29. **How Well Do You Know ... ?** The teacher asks students to submit questions that will help them learn more about a classmate. For example, where were they born? What is their favorite food? What is their favorite TV show? Then the teachers divide the kids into *pair and share* groups. The two students interview each other and report back to the class all about their classmates.

30. **I-Spy.** The teacher identifies a common household object like a fork, a box of cereal, or a sock. The teacher direct messages a student with the I-Spy object of the week and asks them to discreetly make it visible in their Zoom video. Then, the teacher lets the rest of the class know what the object is, and the person who finds it first wins.

31. **Invention Convention.** The teacher holds up two random objects and asks students to combine them into an innovative new invention—for example, fingernail clippers and a tennis ball. The teacher divides students into breakout groups where they brainstorm their inventions and come up with a product name and slogan. The class comes back together in an invention convention to hear about all the ideas.

32. **Jackbox Games.** Jackbox is fun and collaborative gaming that is best suited for older teens with great options for drawing and trivia games. The teacher must have a Jackbox account to share a game over a Zoom feed. Students can join in on almost any device.

33. **Kahoot.** This is a fun way for teachers to run a virtual quiz. It's super easy for kids to join and fun to see the results in real time.

34. **Karaoke.** Zoom Karaoke is as easy as it gets. Students simply take turns looking up karaoke videos and singing them together.

35. **Lightning Scavenger Hunt.** The teacher names a household item and the time allotted for students to go find it. Items could be specific objects like a coffee mug or salt shaker, or personal objects like the "last book you read" or "your favorite snack."

36. **Livestreams of Animals.** Explore.org offers animal livestreams, from birds and bears to wildlife and marine life. To liven it up while students are doing independent work, the teacher can screenshare a live animal camera just for fun.

37. **Paper-Tear Challenge Share.** The teacher poses a simple on-the-spot challenge. For example, the teacher says, "Grab one sheet of paper and close your eyes. Do not open your eyes until I ask you to. First, fold your sheet of paper in half. Second, tear off the upper right-hand corner. Third, fold your paper in half again. Fourth, tear off the lower right-hand corner. Now, fold your paper in half. Tear off the upper left-hand corner. Fold the paper in half a final time. Tear off the lower left-hand corner. Unfold your paper and hold it up. Open your eyes and compare your paper with others." The point of the activity is to show that people can follow the same set of directions and have very different outcomes, and that is creativity.

38. **Mind-meld.** Divide the students into two groups. Group one gives group two a challenge word. Everyone in group two has thirty seconds to write down three words associated with that word. After the thirty seconds, they then hold their papers up to the webcam so everyone can see what they wrote. If there is one word in common in what all players in the team write, they win a point. Repeat for the other team.

39. **Musical Statues.** Before starting, check that everyone has their webcam set up such that you can see them in their "dancing space" and then play musical statues as normal. When the music starts, everyone begins to dance. When the music is stopped, everyone freezes (stops dancing), and the person who is still moving is out of the game. This continues until there is one person left. A great and easy party game for small and big kids.

40. **Mystery Bag.** The teacher holds an object in a mystery bag and reveals three clues or a riddle about what is inside. The whole class has the opportunity to ask no more than ten questions to figure out what is in the bag. The kids work together via chat to ask the very best questions possible to solve the mystery bag.

41. **Mystery Menu.** The teacher puts up pictures of random cooking ingredients. The students brainstorm what menu could be created from these ingredients.

42. **Mystery City.** Students arrive to Zoom like they are arriving at a mystery city. The teacher plays themed music and has a themed virtual background. Students must guess where they are in the world.

43. **Name That Tune.** Prior to the game, the teacher creates a playlist with familiar songs, and students use the chat to guess the title.

This game can also be played with sound effects like animal noises and other recognizable sounds.

44. **Personalized Online Learning Signs.** Signs are great tools for distance learning. The teacher begins by showing students homemade signs that say things like "I have a question" or "I can't hear you" or a sign that flips between "yes" and "no." Then the teacher asks students to think about how they could use signs to interact with both teachers and peers. Finally, using paper or art materials students have at home, each child creates a set of desk signs that can help them express themselves in distance learning.

45. **Picnic Lunch.** The teacher sends the kids outside to find a safe spot for a picnic lunch. Each child takes a photo to share with the class afterward.

46. **Pictionary.** This classic game is easy to play online using the whiteboard app in Zoom. The drawing teammate will receive a prompt. Try an online Pictionary generator. The playing team will have one minute to guess the drawing. If the team does not guess before the minute expires, the other team will have a chance to steal.

47. **Wacky Breakout Clubs.** Save ten minutes at the end of class for students to self-select into a Wacky Breakout Club. These clubs meet only once and give students a fun way to socialize with friends. Think of funny names like Cheetos Club, Mandalorian Club, Untied Sneakers Club, Hoodies All Day Club, and other fun titles. Give each Wacky Breakout Club one entertaining "Would You Rather … ?" question to discuss in breakouts for five minutes. Then the teacher brings all students back together to hear what each group learned.

48. **Record a Podcast.** The teacher divides students into breakout groups and tells them they will be recording live podcasts around a topic or theme. Students divide their roles between host, cohost, and expert guests. Zoom enables recording audio directly on the platform for easy editing later. Ask the students to edit the podcast together, and then invite the whole class to listen to all the different points of view on that topic.

49. **Fake Answers, Real Questions.** The teacher asks students to make up fake answers to real trivia questions and mixes in these answers with the real answer. The students have to find the real answer among the fakes. Teachers can also ask students to make the trivia game.

50. **Pun Challenge.** The teacher picks a category and challenges students to come up with puns.

51. **Reflecting for Relevance.** This Zoom Booster helps students link schoolwork to their real lives. Break the kids into smaller groups, and encourage them to use online infographic creators like Venngage, Canva, Adobe Spark, or Piktochart to find connections between classroom content and modern-day life. Then invite everyone back together to hear, see, and discuss their work.

52. **Remember When.** During the pandemic, this gives kids a way to reminisce together. The first student says, "Remember when … " ("Remember when our class went to the pumpkin patch?"). The next student continues the story by adding a sentence that starts with "Yes! And then … " ("Yes! And then we petted the goats.") Keep going, with each student adding more details.

53. **Rewrite the Lyrics.** Pick a popular song and ask students to rewrite the lyrics to tie into a lesson or theme in the class.

54. **Riddles.** Boost engagement with a riddle break. Search the web for age-appropriate riddles for your class, and then let the kids collaborate to try and solve them.

55. **Rock, Paper, Scissors.** For younger kids, the teacher can read aloud from *The Legend of Rock Paper Scissors* and then invite students to play the game in breakout rooms of three people. Remember, scissors cut paper, paper covers rock, and rock crushes scissors. Students can play with video or by typing their selection using emojis in the chat box.

56. **See. Think. Wonder.** Try using Harvard Project Zero's thinking routines to help kids think about and reflect on their learning. See the whole toolbox of thinking routines here: **pz.harvard.edu/ thinking-routines**.

57. **Simon Says.** In this familiar game, the student or teacher could be Simon and give instructions on actions for the rest of the class to do, making sure to say, "Simon says," before each action. Just like the real game, if other students do the action without hearing "Simon Says," they are out.

58. **Slogan Game.** Search the web for "online slogan game," and then screenshare the logos of well-known companies and try to match the slogan. You could also do this with book covers, dates in history, and other subject-specific content.

59. **Something in Common.** Something in Common connects students around their similarities. Divide the students into breakout groups. For round one, challenge students to find three things they have in common. For round two, challenge students to find the most unique or unusual thing they have in common.

60. **Spin the Wheel.** To make calling on students more interactive, use an online wheel spinner like **www.wheelofnames.com**. Teachers can personalize the wheels with the names of all students in the class or make a custom wheel for any subject or theme.

61. **Spot the Difference.** Show the kids two nearly identical illustrations, and challenge them to find the variations. Assign kids to breakout groups to hunt for differences and make guesses by typing in the chat box. The first player or team to spot all the differences wins a point.

62. **Spirit Days.** At the beginning of each month, post some fun daily themes or spirit days in advance, and encourage students to show enthusiasm by wearing a specific color, a crazy hat, sunglasses, or other ideas. Crowdsource theme day ideas from the students for engagement.

63. **Stretch Breaks.** Use any number of websites to give your students a movement break. Try **www.gonoodle.com**, yoga, tai chi, dance, or just good old jumping jacks.

64. **Student-Led Live Polls.** Zoom's polling feature allows teachers to ask opinions and instantly display results. Students can vote on a question or series of questions in a two-to-four-answer format. Why not change it up and let students develop and lead some interactive polls? Divide the students into breakout groups, and let each group develop and lead a real-time poll.

65. **Surprise Guest.** The teacher announces that a special guest will join the Zoom at a specified time. It could be another teacher, a parent, or someone giving a lesson related to topics or themes in the classroom. Or it could be classmate in disguise or costume. Have fun with it.

66. **Themed Teacher Office Hours.** Many teachers are holding office hours via Zoom but make it more fun for students to attend by creating themed office hours—for example, funny hat office hours, favorite snack office hours, outdoor office hours. This gives teacher and student a point of connection and humor that lightens the mood.

67. **Tongue Twister Challenge.** The teacher shares a tongue twister on the screen and encourages students to practice reading it once or twice before asking for volunteers to read it out loud for fun.

68. **Trivia.** The teacher asks the students to compile trivia questions and answers to use as energy boosters through the day, or the teacher can use a random trivia generator.

69. **Sell It Better.** The teacher screenshares a photo of a common everyday object like a rubber band, a paper clip, or duct tape. The teacher then divides students into smaller breakout groups and gives students instructions to come up with a sales pitch for the object. When the kids come back together, the team that sells it best wins.

70. **Twin Tuesday.** On Monday the teacher assigns each student a partner. Then on Tuesday students show up twinning with their newfound buddy. Points are given for those who match in funny or creative ways. Each pair shares two fun facts about each other.

71. **Two Truths and a Fib.** This is a good icebreaker for collaborative group work. Divide students into breakout groups. One by one, each student shares three things about themselves, two truths and one fib. The other students guess which is the fib.

72. **Virtual Puzzles.** Many websites offer virtual collaborative puzzles. Ravensburger's Puzzle World features some of their most

popular jigsaw puzzles online, and teachers can also opt to create a custom puzzle by uploading a picture. You'll receive a custom URL you can share with students.

73. **Virtual Vacation or Field Trip.** The teacher announces a virtual vacation or field trip! Using screenshare or by sharing links in the chat, the teacher takes the class to a surprise destination like a museum, historical site, or tourist destination. See chapter 4 for a list of ideas.

74. **Visual Brainteasers and Optical Illusions**. Search the web for visual brain teasers and optical illusions. This site is a good place to start: **www.brainden.com/optical-illusions.htm**. The teacher divides students into breakout groups to work together and solve the puzzles. When the groups solve one challenge, give them more challenges to solve.

75. **What's Snacking?** While doing distance learning, many students keep a snack nearby. Do a quick "What's Snacking?" break, and ask students to hold their nearby snacks up for all to see.

76. **Where's Waldo?** Do a Google search for "Where's Waldo Online," and choose a photo that matches your classroom topics or themes. Screenshare the photo and challenge your students to find Waldo on screen.

77. **Who Wins the Bracket?** Come up with a variety of fun categories, and set up tournament brackets. Sample categories could be Best Knock-Knock Joke, Best Snack Food, Best Marvel Superhero, or Best Disney Character. Ask students to vote on each head-to-head competition using Zoom's polling feature. Advance the brackets winner until only one winner is left.

78. **Word Cloud Generators.** Word clouds highlight key themes and show students "trending" topics in a discussion. They're fun, engaging, and updating in real-time as students' comments are added to the discussion. Try **www.acadly.com**, which integrates with Zoom, or many other word cloud generators like **www.wordclouds.com**, **www.wordart.com**, **www.worditout.com**, or **www.wordle.com**.

79. **Word Games.** For a play break, teachers can bring virtual Scrabble, Words with Friends, Boggle, and Serpentine into the online classroom. There are many online variations to choose from.

80. **Yes, Let's!** The teacher starts by saying, "Let's _____" with a suggestion for something the whole class can do together, like salute, clap hands, or spin around. The teacher instructs everyone else to reply with, "Yes, let's!" and then do the corresponding action together for a few seconds. Next, a student suggests a new action, and the pattern continues.

As you think of more ideas for distance learning engagement, write them down and share them with others. We're all in this together!

APPENDIX VI: THE WONDER APPROACH TO PORTFOLIO MAKING

There is no right or wrong way for your child to make a portfolio. I've provided this approach to get your creative juices flowing. Have fun!

How Do You Do It? With WONDER

Divide your portfolio into the following sections. You can add or delete or customize these sections based on your own preferences, but this is a good place to start.

1. **W**ho You Are

2. **O**riginal Work

3. **N**ew Areas of Interest

4. **D**iversity of All Kinds

5. **E**xperiences

6. **R**ecommendations

W: WHO YOU ARE

This section is a bio that tells the story of your child and their growth. It brings to life who they are as a person, not just as a student. Here are some questions your child can ask themself as they get started:

- What makes me unique and different?

- What are my passions, talents, interests, and skills?

- What are the most exciting and defining things about me as a person?

- What aspects of my sense of humor stand out?

- Do I have a unique vision of the world or the future?

- Am I passionately curious about topics, issues, or subjects?

- How have I most changed through childhood and adolescence?

- How do the people closest to me describe my strengths?

This section is the attention-grabbing introduction, so be creative! Once you have a sense of the content to include, brainstorm with your child how they can design an introduction that sets them apart. It could be a video—like the Sprite guy, an infographic, a cleverly-worded brochure, a recipe, a sketch, a mock article, or a bio presented as personalized nutrition information on the back of cereal box. The sky is the limit for creativity here, so take some time with your child to imagine a clever idea that brings their unique story to life. You'll notice certain things are not included in this section, including grades, GPA, and SAT scores. These things can be added into later sections.

O: ORIGINAL WORK

One of the primary roles of a personal portfolio is to show off what your child can *do*, inside and outside school. Encourage your child to think about their skills, talents, experiences, and accomplishments. Don't be shy about flaunting how what they have done has huge value. Keep in mind the invisible skills that are not graded on a report card, such as good judgment, kindness, emotional intelligence, good listening, strong sense of responsibility, practical financial skills, critical-thinking and problem-solving skills, teamwork and collaboration, foreign languages, video editing, skill in storytelling, leadership, and willingness and ability to help their peers—to name just a few. Now encourage your child to find examples of work they have done (inside or outside school) that demonstrate these things in action.

Some examples of this might be:

- An essay or research paper (or an excerpt from one)
- A video of a speech they gave
- A piece of artwork
- A recording of a song they performed (or a song they wrote!)
- Documentation of a science experiment they conducted
- Photos of something they built, repaired, or renovated
- A short film they made
- A clip from a play they acted in or directed
- A logo they designed for a team
- A poster they designed for an event
- Photos of a recipe they prepared
- Examples of volunteer work
- Examples of summer camps or workshops they participated in
- Sample daily schedule of workouts or study habits
- Examples of interactions at Boys & Girls Clubs or other service organization
- Pictures from races and fundraising events
- Babysitting or caring for an elderly relative

Tell how your child completed this work, whether it is tangible or not. Describe the goals for project-based activities, how they came up with the solution, the tools or methods they used, the obstacles they overcame, the lessons learned, the skills gained, the benefits of the result, and more. Include activities that are not project-specific as well, such as unique family responsibilities.

N: NEW AREAS OF INTEREST

Colleges, employers, internship directors, and other types of organizations want to invest in people who invest in themselves. In this section, your child can give someone a peek into their emerging curiosities and how they hope to proactively create their own bright future. Here is where your child demonstrates that their learning journey is not defined just by the school curriculum.

Start by talking to your child about their biggest and boldest dreams and visions for the future. Now ask your child about what they need to learn, do, or think about to proactively take steps toward these things. How do they see these things changing or evolving as they learn and grow?

Ask them:

- What are you most curious about?

- What are you most excited about?

- What do you really want to do that you haven't done yet?

- What are the greatest things you want to accomplish, if you had unlimited time and resources?

- If you could do anything you wanted with your life, no limits, what would it be?

- What do you wish you could change about the world?

- What do you want to contribute to the world?

- What steps can you take to do these things?

Once again, think about how to share all of this in a creative way. Brainstorm with your child about the value they bring to a school, company, team, or organization, because he or she is thinking ahead and learning new things. Think about how much energy and excitement your child will bring to the room when people know that he or she is proactively taking steps in their own direction. Can this energy be translated into a video, a cartoon, a song?

D: DIVERSITY OF ALL KINDS

So many college admission teams complain that many applications feel the same. They seek diversity, not only in types of people, but in types of thinking, doing, acting, and being. This section allows your child to showcase their diversity. Talk about things like culture, upbringing, and family traditions. Share your child's diversity of interests, talents, ideas, friends, and efforts. Here your child can show their curiosities, explorations, and passion projects—even quirky ones. Here is where your child can stand out as a diverse thinker who comes at the world with their own perspectives and knowledge base.

Feature your child's participation in any groups or organizations. If they attend church, Scouts, foreign language school, volunteering, et cetera, put it in the portfolio. The same goes for any clubs and social groups—whether it's chess club, drama club, an a cappella group, or a weekly Settlers of Catan game your child participates in (or runs!).

This is also a great way to show how your child applies skills to "real life" as well as working on a team and on projects—which can add up to real experience.

Many scholarships and awards require evidence of your child's community involvement. Consider your child's involvement in the following:

- Driver's education courses

- First aid/CPR courses

- Cultural clubs/organizations

- Religious groups

- Fundraising events

- Other activities specific to your community

- Boys & Girls Clubs or other mentorship groups

- Clubs and social groups

E: EXPERIENCES

This is where your child describes both their greatest successes and their toughest challenges.

Greatest Successes

I would challenge you to expand this definition to include not just the projects where the end results turned out the best, but also proudest moments, biggest wins, biggest lessons learned, and biggest turning points or revelations. Remember that success doesn't just mean a good grade or even a project that turned out perfectly! An experience in which your child learned an important lesson or discovered a new passion is equally valuable.

For each "I did it!" entry, include a very clear case for why it made the list. This description can include what your child did, how they did it, methods used, obstacles overcome, lessons learned, skills gained, benefits, and how it contributed to where they are today. To make this section even stronger, tie these "successes" into how they encourage your child to dream big and reach for the stars. Encourage your child to connect successes to their big dreams and visions from the "New Areas of Interest" section.

Toughest Challenges

One way your child can really stand out is to explain their toughest challenges and how they overcame them. It's very insightful to learn what someone defines as a tough challenge, and it's very revealing to hear how a person leverages their problem-solving skills, strength, and grit to overcome it.

For this section, talk with your child about when they faced a tough situation. This could be a situation at school, at an extracurricular activity, in their personal life; it could be an academic problem, a social problem, a personal problem. Have them recount how they used their inner strength, skills, and creativity to find solutions. If at all possible, look for challenges that relate to those big dreams and visions, and connect the lessons learned to their movement forward toward their future.

For both of these, find a way to creatively tell the stories, through words, pictures, a story, a video, or a combination of multiple mediums. Encourage your child to paint a picture of what they are like when they feel at their best—under both great and tough circumstances.

R: RECOMMENDATIONS

This is the section traditionally thought of as a "recommendation letter." A recommendation is usually a written statement of reference prepared by someone who knows your child. Often these letters come across as formulaic and generalized, and they rarely make your child jump off the page. They are often written long after the child has finished the class, project, or activity they worked on with this person, so the letter writer is often pulling from half-forgotten memories instead of their immediate experience with your child.

This is why the formal recommendation letter is dying. Why would your child wait until the end of four years of high school to get people to reflect on their areas of strength? Timely recommendations are more relevant to the nonlinear ways in which we live and work.

So, rather than the traditional kind of recommendation letter, think of this recommendation as more of an endorsement. An endorsement is when someone specifically validates and confirms some aspect of your child's portfolio. It could be a skill endorsement, a talent endorsement, a mindset endorsement, but it is specific and supportive of the story in the portfolio.

As your child enjoys a success, overcomes a challenge, participates in a unique group or organization, pursues a new area of interest, or creates an original work, ask someone involved to write an endorsement. It does not have to be long; it just needs to speak to the skill, talent, mindset, enthusiasm, learning, curiosity, or another specific aspect of your child's experience. Also include a picture of your child and their endorser together! (And yes, this can be a screenshot if they are working together over Zoom or another virtual platform!) Just make sure you get permission to feature the endorsement and photo in your child's portfolio.

Lastly, make sure your child sends a thank-you letter to each of these people.

Optional: Academic Record and Personal Reflection on My Academic Record

Finally, encourage your child to feature their academic record last.

Why last? Because, as we've discussed, it is a traditional measure of success and will do absolutely nothing to help your child stand out. If you simply can't break with tradition and feel compelled to include your child's latest report card and transcript, encourage your child to bring it to life with an annotated reflection on what lies behind the grades. Tie the grades back to specific projects, experiences, lessons, et cetera, already included in the portfolio. If you must include it, make it relevant and meaningful.

How to Format the Portfolio

In short, be creative! Remember the Sprite guy?

Talk with your child about formatting the portfolio so it is easy for someone else to read and understand the information but is also attention-grabbing and entertaining. Make sure that the things you are most proud of stand out loud and clear. And have fun!

And speaking of creativity: If you don't like the WONDER acronym—feel free to come up with your own!

ENDNOTES

1   Odyssey of the Mind is a worldwide creative problem-solving competition started in 1978. Learn more about the program online at www.odysseyofthemind.com.

2   Rebecca Winthrop, "COVID-19 and School Closures: What Can Countries Learn from Past Emergencies?" *Brookings* (blog), March 31, 2020, https://www.brookings.edu/research/covid-19-and-school-closures-what-can-countries-learn-from-past-emergencies/.

3   George Psacharopoulos, Harry A. Patrinos, Victoria Collis, and Emiliana Vegas, "The COVID-19 Cost of School Closures," World Bank Blogs (blog), April 30, 2020, https://blogs.worldbank.org/education/covid-19-cost-school-closures.

4   Laura Camera, "As Many As 3 Million Children Have Gone Without Education Since March: Estimate," *US News & World Report*, October 21, 2020, https://www.usnews.com/news/education-news/articles/2020-10-21/as-many-as-3-million-children-have-gone-without-education-since-march-estimate.

5   Howard Markel, "Analysis: Why Some Schools Stayed Open during the 1918 Flu Pandemic," *PBS NewsHour*, July 13, 2020, https://www.pbs.org/newshour/health/analysis-why-some-schools-stayed-open-during-the-1918-flu-pandemic.

6   Chris Butler, "Rutherford County Schools Tell Parents Not to Monitor Their Child's Virtual Classrooms," *The Tennessee Star*, August 15, 2020, https://tennesseestar.com/2020/08/15/rutherford-county-schools-tell-parents-not-to-monitor-their-childs-virtual-classrooms/.

7   Anna Kamenetz, "A Rising Number Of U.S. Children Have The Option Of In-Person School," NPR, October 22, 2020, https://www.npr.org/sections/coronavirus-live-updates/2020/10/22/926757172/a-rising-number-of-u-s-children-have-the-option-of-in-person-school.

8   "The Importance of Reopening America's Schools This Fall," Centers for Disease Control and Prevention, July 23, 2020, https://www.cdc.gov/coronavirus/2019-ncov/community/schools-childcare/reopening-schools.html.

9   Sandra L. Hofferth and John F. Sandberg, "Changes in American Children's Time, 1981–1997," *Advances in Life Course Research, Children at the Millennium* 6 (January 1, 2001): 193–229, https://doi.org/10.1016/S1040-2608(01)80011-3.

10 Sandra L. Hofferth, "Changes in American Children's Time—1997 to 2003," *Electronic International Journal of Time Use Research* 6, no. 1 (January 1, 2009): 26–47.

11 Stephen L. Brown, Brandye D. Nobiling, James Teufel, and David A. Birch, "Are Kids Too Busy?: Early Adolescents' Perceptions of Discretionary Activities, Overscheduling, and Stress," *The Journal of School Health* 81, no. 9 (September 2011): 574–80, https://doi.org/10.1111/j.1746-1561.2011.00629.x.

12 A. Toffler, *Future Shock* (New York: Random House, 1970).

13 Arooj Ahmed, "The Rate of Content Consumption Immensely Increased during the Coronavirus Pandemic," Digital Information World (blog), October 1, 2020, https://www.digitalinformationworld.com/2020/10/the-rate-of-content-consumption-immensely-increased-during-the-coronavirus-pandemic.html.

14 Trevor Haynes, "Dopamine, Smartphones & You: A Battle For Your Time," Harvard University: The Graduate School of Arts & Sciences (blog), May 1, 2018, http://sitn.hms.harvard.edu/flash/2018/dopamine-smartphones-battle-time/.

15 "Addictive Behaviours: Gaming Disorder," World Health Organization (WHO), September 14, 2018, https://www.who.int/news-room/q-a-detail/addictive-behaviours-gaming-disorder.

16 Mary Helen Immordino-Yang, Joanna A. Christodoulou, and Vanessa Singh, "Rest Is Not Idleness: Implications of the Brain's Default Mode for Human Development and Education," *Perspectives on Psychological Science* 7, no. 4 (June 29, 2012), https://doi.org/10.1177/1745691612447308.

17 Tim Kreider, "ANXIETY; The 'Busy' Trap," *The New York Times*, July 1, 2012, https://archive.nytimes.com/query.nytimes.com/gst/fullpage-940DEED8113AF932A35754C0A9649D8B63.html.

18 Alyssa Fowers, "Last Year, We Searched Google for How to Tie a Tie. Now We're Using It to Find Toilet Paper," *Washington Post*, April 17, 2020, https://www.washingtonpost.com/business/2020/04/17/last-year-we-searched-google-how-tie-tie-now-were-using-it-find-toilet-paper/.

19 Todd Kashdan, "5 Benefits of Curiosity," ExperienceLife, December 1, 2019, https://experiencelife.com/article/the-power-of-curiosity/.

20 Todd B. Kashdan, *Curious? Discover the Missing Ingredient to a Fulfilling Life*, reprint edition (New York: Harper Perennial, 2010).

21 Daniel T. Willingham, *Why Don't Students Like School?: A Cognitive Scientist Answers Questions About How the Mind Works and What It Means for the Classroom* (San Francisco, CA: Jossey-Bass, 2010).

22 Sophie von Stumm, Benedikt Hell, and Tomas Chamorro-Premuzic, "The Hungry Mind: Intellectual Curiosity Is the Third Pillar of Academic Performance," *Perspectives on Psychological Science* 6, no. 6 (November 1, 2011): 574–88, https://doi.org/10.1177/1745691611421204.

23   Matthias J. Gruber, Bernard D. Gelman, and Charan Ranganath, "States of Curiosity Modulate Hippocampus-Dependent Learning via the Dopaminergic Circuit," *Neuron* 84, no. 2 (October 22, 2014): 486–96, https://doi.org/10.1016/j.neuron.2014.08.060.

24   Teresa Amabile, Constance Noonan Hadley, and Steven J. Kramer, "Creativity Under the Gun," *Harvard Business Review*, August 1, 2002, https://hbr.org/2002/08/creativity-under-the-gun.

25   Scott Sorokin, "Thriving in a World of 'Knowledge Half-Life,'" CIO, April 5, 2019, https://www.cio.com/article/3387637/thriving-in-a-world-of-knowledge-half-life.html.

26   The Great Courses Plus. https://www.thegreatcoursesplus.com/.

27   Jayme Kinsey, "5 Worst Messy Trees for the Lazy Landscaper," *Dengarden—Home and Garden* (blog), November 28, 2019, https://dengarden.com/landscaping/5-Worst-Trees-For-The-Lazy-Landscaper.

28   Brent Frantz, "Sweetgum Balls and Tamiflu," *Bag-A-Nut* (blog), March 28, 2019, https://baganut.com/blogs/news/sweetgum-balls-and-tamiflu.

29   Todd Kashdan, "5 Benefits of Curiosity," ExperienceLife, December 1, 2019, https://experiencelife.com/article/the-power-of-curiosity/.

30   Dan Rothstein, "Setting Off Sparks of Curiosity and Creativity," Harvard Graduate School of Education, February 3, 2012, https://www.gse.harvard.edu/news/12/02/setting-sparks-curiosity-and-creativity.

31   Daisy Yuhas, "Piqued: The Case for Curiosity," *The Hechinger Report*, June 27, 2018, https://hechingerreport.org/piqued-the-case-for-curiosity/.

32   Michael Brice-Saddler, "From Cooking to Calligraphy, People Stuck at Home Are Finding New Space for Creativity," *Washington Post*, April 11, 2020, https://www.washingtonpost.com/nation/2020/04/11/cooking-calligraphy-people-stuck-home-are-finding-new-space-creativity/.

33   Google Trends search, November 1, 2020.

34   Jewel, "Grateful," *The Call to Unite*, 2020, https://unite.us/video-gallery/fj1ti2sqfge0wiic81ncpldfdqjakn.

35   The Nature Conservancy, "Children These Days: Why Is America's Youth Staying Indoors?" *Children & Nature Network* (blog), September 12, 2011, https://www.childrenandnature.org/2011/09/12/children_these_days_why_is_americas_youth_staying_indoors/.

36   "Whole Child: Developing Mind, Body and Spirit through Outdoor Play," National Wildlife Federation, August 2010.

37   Katherine Martinko, "Children Spend Less Time Outside Than Prison Inmates," Treehugger, October 11, 2018, https://www.treehugger.com/children-spend-less-time-outside-prison-inmates-4857353.

38   Florence Williams, "Call to the Wild: This Is Your Brain on Nature," *National Geographic*, January 2016, https://www.nationalgeographic.com/magazine/2016/01/call-to-wild/.

39   "Whole Child: Developing Mind, Body and Spirit through Outdoor Play," National Wildlife Federation, August 2010.

40   University of East Anglia, "It's Official—Spending Time Outside Is Good for You," ScienceDaily, July 6, 2018, https://www.sciencedaily.com/releases/2018/07/180706102842.htm.

41   Cat Wise and Jason Kane, "Why Doctors Are Increasingly Prescribing Nature," *PBS NewsHour*, August 28, 2019, https://www.pbs.org/newshour/show/why-doctors-are-increasingly-prescribing-nature.

42   Alan Ewert and Yun Chang, "Levels of Nature and Stress Response," *Behavioral Sciences* 8, no. 5 (May 17, 2018), https://doi.org/10.3390/bs8050049.

43 "It's Official—Spending Time Outside Is Good for You," University of East Anglia, July 6, 2018.

44 Florence Williams, "Call to the Wild: This Is Your Brain on Nature," *National Geographic*, January 2016, https://www.nationalgeographic.com/magazine/2016/01/call-to-wild/.

45 Jason Hreha, "Be A Creator, Not A Consumer," Medium, June 9, 2017, https://medium.com/@jhreha/be-a-creator-not-a-consumer-ceb7cddd97ca.

46 Shivangi Dhawan, "Online Learning: A Panacea in the Time of COVID-19 Crisis," *Journal of Educational Technology Systems* 49, no. 1 (September 1, 2020): 5–22.

47 Joshua Block, "Embracing Messy Learning," George Lucas Educational Foundation: *Edutopia* (blog), January 7, 2014, https://www.edutopia.org/blog/embracing-messy-learning-joshua-block.

48 Adam White, "'She's the E.T. That He Couldn't Put in His Films': Steven Spielberg's Eccentric Mother Leah Adler Dies at 97," *The Telegraph*, February 22, 2017, https://www.telegraph.co.uk/films/0/steven-spielbergs-eccentric-mother-leah-adler-dies-97/.

49 S. Moser, "Mind Your Errors: Evidence for a Neural Mechanism Linking Growth Mind-Set to Adaptive Posterror Adjustments," *Psychological Science* 22 no. 12 (2011): 1484–1489, https://doi.org/10.1177/0956797611419520.

50 "The Future of Jobs Report 2020," World Economic Forum, October 20, 2020, https://www.weforum.org/reports/the-future-of-jobs-report-2020/.

51 Katie White, *Unlocked: Assessment as the Key to Everyday Creativity in the Classroom* (Bloomington, IN: Solution Tree Press, 2019).

52   Stephen Noonoo, "The Greatest Enemy of Creativity in Schools Isn't Testing. It's Time," EdSurge, December 18, 2018, https://www. edsurge.com/news/2018-12-18-the-greatest-enemy-of-creativity-in-schools-isn-t-testing-it-s-time.

53   Ken Robinson, "Do Schools Kill Creativity?" TED Talk, filmed February 2006, video, 19:14, https://www.ted.com/talks/ sir_ken_robinson_do_schools_kill_creativity?language=en.

54   Kelly McSweeney, "The Left-Brain Right-Brain Myth: Is It True?" Now, Powered by Northrop Grumman, April 26, 2018, https://now. northropgrumman.com/the-left-brain-right-brain-myth-is-it-true/.

55   Kyung Hee Kim, "The Creativity Crisis: The Decrease in Creative Thinking Scores on the Torrance Tests of Creative Thinking," *Creativity Research Journal* 23, no. 4 (October 1, 2011): 285–95.

56   Kim, "Creativity Crisis," 292.

57   Ibid.

58   Clifton B. Parker, "Stanford Research Shows Pitfalls of Homework," Stanford News, March 10, 2014, https://news.stanford.edu/2014/03/10/ too-much-homework-031014/.

      For more on the homework problem, see these two great books: Alfie Kohn, *The Homework Myth: Why Our Kids Get Too Much of a Bad Thing* (Cambridge, MA: Da Capo Lifelong Books, 2007); and Sara Bennett and Nancy Kalish, *The Case Against Homework: How Homework Is Hurting Children and What Parents Can Do About It* (New York: Harmony, 2007).

59   Kohn, *The Homework Myth*.

60   Jennifer Earl, "Second-grade teacher's unique homework policy goes viral," CBSNews.com, August 24, 2016, https://www.cbsnews.com/ news/second-grade-teachers-unique-homework-policy-goes-viral/.

61   "Carol Dweck: A Summary of Growth and Fixed Mindsets," *Farnam Street* (blog), https://fs.blog/2015/03/carol-dweck-mindset/.

62   Matt Soniak, "How Come You Never Got An 'E' in School?" Mental Floss, June 18, 2010, https://www.mentalfloss.com/article/24960/how-come-you-never-got-e-school.

63   "Montgomery County's Grade Inflation Should Be a Wake-up Call: When More and More Students Get A's, Real Accomplishments Aren't Being Measured," *Washington Post*, October 7, 2018, https://www.washingtonpost.com/opinions/montgomery-countys-grade-inflation-should-be-a-wake-up-call/2018/10/07/e5ab3844-c74f-11e8-b1ed-1d2d65b86d0c_story.html.

64   Chase Zreet, "The Big Dumb Thing," http://www.chasezreet.com/thespriteguy.

65   Tim Nudd, "How a Copywriter's Amazing Tribute to Sprite Got Him Hired at W+K," *Adweek*, March 13, 2018, https://www.adweek.com/agencies/how-a-copywriters-amazing-tribute-to-sprite-got-him-hired-at-wk/.

66   Peter McInerney, "Toward a Critical Pedagogy of Engagement for Alienated Youth: Insights from Freire and School-based Research," *Critical Studies in Education* 50, no. 1 (February 1, 2009): 23–35.

67   Judy Willis, "Where Did the Joy of Learning Go?" *Psychology Today* (blog), December 19, 2015, https://www.psychologytoday.com/us/blog/radical-teaching/201512/where-did-the-joy-learning-go.

68   J. Willis, "The Neuroscience of Joyful Education," *Educational Leadership*, ASCD 64, 2007.

69   Ibid.

CPSIA information can be obtained
at www.ICGtesting.com
Printed in the USA
JSHW032339080421
13393JS00007B/156